# WILD IN LONDON

*for Diana*

First published in Great Britain by Michael Joseph Ltd
27 Wrights Lane, London W8
1986

*British Library Cataloguing in Publication Data*
Goode, David
Wild in London.
1. Nature conservation——England——London
I. Title
639.9'09421    QH77.G7
ISBN 0–7181–2518–5 (Hardback)
ISBN 0–7181–2729–3 (Paperback)

Typeset in Linotron 202 Sabon by Wilmaset, Birkenhead, Wirral
Printed and bound by Mondadori, Italy

# WILD IN LONDON

## DAVID GOODE

*with photography by*
*Chris Schwarz*

MICHAEL JOSEPH LONDON
A SHELL BOOK

ACKNOWLEDGEMENTS I would like to thank all who have provided information and ideas, including my colleagues in the Greater London Council, and members of natural history and conservation bodies in London. In particular, thanks go to Leo Batten, Audley Gosling, Max Nicholson, Peter Edwards and Pam Morris for permission to use unpublished material. Thanks are also due to Douglas Kite, Katie Melville, Bernard Bligh, Brian Mist, Anne Mayo, John Newton, Ros Brewer, Joyce Bellamy, Warwick Reynolds and Peter Creasey for information about particular aspects of London's natural history; also to Gina Douglas, the librarian of the Linnean Society for her willing assistance. I would also like to thank all those whom I met and talked to on my travels around London, including many early morning visitors to places such as Wimbledon Common, Queens Wood and Walthamstow Marsh. I hope some of their enthusiasm for London's wildlife is reflected in the book. A big thankyou also to Mrs Olive Ward for several evenings of badger watching at her home.

I wish to thank the Department of the Environment for permission to photograph wildlife in the Royal Parks; Thames Water for permission to visit the herony at Walthamstow and many of their water works and reservoirs; and British Rail for permission to visit various pieces of disused railway land.

Thanks are also due to Shell UK for their contribution on behalf of the Better Britain Campaign but I should emphasise that the views expressed are my own.
Particular thanks are due to Jennifer Davis for typing the manuscript; to Jacklyn Chandler for her helpful comments on the text and to Jennie Davies, Henrietta Heald and Julia Lilauwala at Michael Joseph for the skill they brought to editing and design. I would also like to thank the photographers who helped to fill gaps in our coverage of nature in London.

Finally I would like to thank my wife Diana for her help, inspiration and support throughout.

---

The places described in this book are only some of the many which are of value to wildlife. It is a personal selection and the absence of other places does not mean that they are less important. A few of the places are private and some can be visited by permission of the owner but the vast majority are freely accessible. However, readers should be aware of the laws of trespass.

# CONTENTS

# INTRODUCTION

LONDON IS ONE of the great capital cities of the world. Created over the centuries, it is now both a monument to past endeavours and a vast, functional, living metropolis with a human population of nearly seven million. But within this huge conglomeration of bricks and mortar, which now extends over 600 square miles, man is not the sole inhabitant.

Even in the most heavily built-up districts something of the natural world can still be seen. In Oxford Street, amidst the hubbub of traffic, it is possible to watch a heron wending its lonely way over the rooftops to fish in the Serpentine. In the Strand one might see a kestrel carrying prey to its nest above the law courts. Rail commuters who travel through Bermondsey to Charing Cross pass a patch of bulrushes growing on a factory roof. Those using the District Line tube near Gunnersbury may notice natural birch and willow woodland where willow warblers sing in May. Some regular travellers know where to spot foxes on the railway embankments. Others enjoy seeing the first primroses of spring or, later, the swathes of deep-red rosebay willowherb covering the banks. The more discerning may even find liverworts and lichens growing on a station platform or hear the intermittent song of a black redstart between the rush of trains at Clapham Junction. Travellers waiting for the tube may well see house mice foraging on the tracks at several of the central London stations, even in the rush hour.

The total wealth of wildlife in and around London is very considerable. Over 100 different kinds of birds nest in Greater London, and as many again are seen regularly in the winter or during periods of migration. Plant life too abounds. About 2000 different sorts of plants are known to grow in the wild within 20 miles of St Paul's. Some are restricted to surviving areas of woodland, marsh, meadow or heath, but others occur in the wide array of artificial habitats which can be found throughout the capital.

London has expanded rapidly since the early nineteenth century from a relatively small and closely confined city to the sprawling metropolis of today. As the city's tentacles have spread, they have engulfed numerous outlying villages and even small towns. Much of the countryside which originally surrounded London has been replaced by urban development. In 1830, Highgate, Hampstead, Fulham and Dulwich were all encircled by rural land which is now part of the inner suburbs. But, fortunately, the process of urbanisation has not been complete. Numerous fragments of the original countryside remain. Woods, river valleys, heaths and commons – even farmland, with hedges, ponds and ditches – can still be found among the twentieth-century suburbs.

Hampstead Heath, Dulwich Woods, Wimbledon Common and Walthamstow Marsh are a few surviving examples of the natural enclaves which once occurred widely in the London area. Such places have great significance. Not only do they maintain links with the past, but they continue to provide the special conditions necessary for the survival of a host of plants and animals. Vestiges of the original woodland cover of London, such as Sydenham Hill and Dulwich Woods or Ruislip Wood, are likely still to contain woodland plants such as yellow archangel, wood anemone and sweet woodruff. Some of these ancient woods may also offer the right habitat for the rarer woodland birds and insects. Similarly, heathlands provide the necessary habitat for stonechats and tree pipits; while redshanks and yellow wagtails are dependent on the few remaining areas of grazing marsh or wet meadowland. So, where these long-established habitats still exist, the more unusual plants and animals may often be found, sometimes even in close proximity to houses and factories.

For town dwellers these fragments of ancient woods, marshes, meadows and heaths offer a real sense of the countryside. But it also has to be said that most natural habitats have suffered as a result of being enclosed within London. For some, the pressures have been too great and the more sensitive species have been lost; others have gradually dwindled. One of the main problems has been that, once they were surrounded by suburbia, natural habitats were no longer managed in traditional ways. Hay cutting, grazing and coppicing were vital to perpetuate particular conditions; when these stopped, many species could not survive. But there are other, more obvious reasons for the decline in London's wildlife. For much of this century, air pollution has had a seriously detrimental influence. Also, the city's huge population, many of whom wish to enjoy its open spaces, has undoubtedly affected the survival of rarer or more sensitive plants and animals. Perhaps too the very fragmentation and isolation of natural places within urban areas has led to the gradual decline of more unusual species.

Whatever its causes, the trend has favoured the ordinary and common species at the expense of the fragile and rare. But it is not surprising to find that even the hardiest of natural habitats are ill fitted to the pressures of city life. The miracle is that they have survived at all.

At the same time, other things have happened to more than compensate for the gradual loss of natural habitats. A great variety of plants and animals have colonised the artificial environments which we have created. This aspect of London's ecology is positive and exciting. Looking round the capital, one cannot but be impressed by the way that nature has taken over in all sorts of places, exploiting new opportunities wherever possible. A gardener's perpetual battle against weeds is one familiar indication of the power of this invasive force. It was well demonstrated in the 1940s too, when wartime bomb sites were rapidly colonised by rosebay willowherb, coltsfoot, Oxford ragwort, sowthistle and Canadian fleabane. This dramatic transformation was largely due to the effective distribution of seeds by wind. But where the occasional bomb sites still remain these original colonisers have long since been replaced by more permanent growths of buddleia, and even by scrub woodland of sycamore or ash.

*The city seen from Hampstead Heath.*

There are 23 square miles of derelict and disused land in London. Some derelict sites have been lying unused for many years and have become veritable nature reserves. The disused railway marshalling yards at Feltham and the old Woolwich Arsenal near Thamesmead are both full of unusual plants to fascinate the botanist. Other derelict industrial sites like docklands, gasworks and even old quarries all have their own particular brand of natural history. Some long- abandoned sewage works and water-treatment plants have been colonised over the years by species which favour wetland habitats and now have a real wilderness quality; in the old filterbeds by Lea Bridge in Hackney, for example, kingfishers, herons and snipe can be seen in what is otherwise a very densely built-up area.

But it is not only the derelict sites which attract wildlife. Many man-made features of London now sustain a considerable proportion of its nature. The extensive flooded gravel pits and reservoirs around the edge of the city provide habitats for a remarkable range of waterfowl; indeed, the London area is now extremely popular for winter birdwatching. Railway embankments are important refuges for many species, and some are even managed as nature reserves. Parks, golf courses, cemeteries and playing fields all cater for wildlife which would otherwise be absent from heavily built-up areas. Suburban gardens, too, contribute enormously to the variety and number of birds to be seen in London. Even buildings which are in constant use play their part by providing suitable conditions for jackdaws, swifts, house martins and kestrels; some, perhaps unbeknown to their occupants, may even be crucial to the survival of colonies of bats.

*Red poppies and ox-eye daisies brighten an area of waste ground by a factory in SE8.*

One particularly interesting development is that some species seem to be becoming better adapted to life in the big city. Take kestrels, for example. When W. H. Hudson wrote his book *Birds in London* in 1898, he thought it unlikely that the kestrel would ever return to the city. But now they are a fairly common sight, even in central areas, and seem to have become successful urban predators. Apparently these town birds have learned the knack of catching house sparrows – in contrast to their country cousins, which feed more exclusively on voles and insects, and only rarely on birds. Another recent incomer to the city is the fox, which has firmly established itself during the past thirty years and is now at home even in the inner suburbs. A further obvious change during this century has been the increase of both gulls and waterfowl. As with the foxes, various species of seagull have adapted to an urban lifestyle for much of the year, and many thousands now spend the winter in the capital.

So there have been some quite surprising increases in the wildlife of London during this century, which are part of a continuously developing pattern. More enlightened human attitudes towards wildlife may also have been an important factor in allowing such increases to occur. When gulls first started to appear along the Thames in the late nineteenth century, they were shot at from London Bridge. But bird-protection laws introduced at about that time have gradually taken effect, and now there is a considerable degree of legal safeguard for birds, plants and various groups of animals, including badgers and bats.

Protection by law is not the only aspect of changing attitudes. During the postwar period in Britain there has been a remarkable growth of interest in nature. The popularity of many wildlife programmes on television is just one indication of this. The burgeoning membership of the Royal Society for the Protection of Birds, which is now approaching half a million, is another. A lot of people are interested not only in nature itself but in protecting natural areas. This is not, of course, entirely new; great battles were fought in the last century to protect Epping Forest and Hampstead Heath. What is different about recent developments is that many more people are involving themselves in local issues. They are concerned to protect nature in the place where they live, and that includes some of the most deprived areas of London. No longer is nature conservation connected solely with the countryside. It has become part of a new approach to life in cities – not only in London but also in many other large cities – and this could well have its roots in a deep-seated desire for greater contact with the natural world.

At a practical level, local people have mounted campaigns to save places which they value, such as Gunnersbury Triangle, a woodland between the railways in Chiswick, and Barnsbury Wood, a small copse entirely surrounded by houses in Islington. Alternatively, the local wildlife patch in need of saving might be a railway embankment in Lewisham, or even a derelict coalyard covered in buddleia bushes at the back of King's Cross station. This is grassroots conservation which depends on the dedication and enthusiasm of local people, many of whom may have had little previous contact with nature.

In some parts of London there is not much wildlife to protect – and there the essential ingredient of nature conservation is creativity. Numerous examples demonstrate that fascinating wildlife habitats can be created by natural colonisation in totally artificial conditions. If so, why shouldn't new wildlife habitats be created by design? It is a matter of making the most of the opportunities that exist. Obviously we can learn a

*Low tide by Waterloo Bridge.* David Goode

lot from studying the wildlife that has already been successful in urban areas; plenty of clues can be found in the natural colonisation of derelict buildings and wasteland. Even the oddities, like bulrushes on a factory roof, offer food for thought.

There is no doubt that many people find inspiration and enjoyment in the rich variety of wild nature now existing in London. It also seems that, even in official circles, a more sympathetic attitude is being adopted to wildlife within the urban scene. But sympathy and acceptance will only go so far. A great deal more is possible. All over London there are places where more of the natural world could be accommodated. But this means catering for nature in a more positive way than has been in evidence hitherto, rather than simply taking for granted what has happened in the past by chance. New and exciting prospects are in view. If they are approached with enthusiasm and care, life could be made more fulfilling for many city dwellers, cut off as they are from the natural world, so that they hardly even notice the passage of the seasons.

◆ ONE ◆

# VESTIGES OF THE NATURAL WORLD

# ◆ WOODLANDS ◆

A ROBIN'S PLAINTIVE song heralded the start of the dawn chorus in Queen's Wood early one chilly April morning. At four thirty it was pitch dark. The sound of heavy lorries could be heard not far away on Archway Road, but the wood was full of natural sounds. A stiff breeze blew through the bare branches of the oaks, rattling the twigs and causing creaks and groans. The robin sang by the only lamp post, along the path to Shepherd's Hill. For some time tawny owls had been calling, their hoots and sharp cries echoing through the trees. Then, just before five o'clock, a wren suddenly struck up with its powerful trill and a blackcap burst into song nearby. Within minutes song thrushes, blackbirds, great tits and blue tits were all singing; the single robin was now accompanied by a multitude of its kind.

A nasal honking from above announced a pair of crows flapping low over the treetops, dark shapes that were difficult to make out against the sky. Ten minutes later it began to lighten in the east. Owls still called, but dawn was breaking and with it came a fine view across London with a silver ribbon of water, the Thames, far in the distance. By now there was bedlam in the wood, with countless tits, thrushes, blackbirds and robins singing furiously. A jay called; a harsh sound among all these songsters. The silvery song of a treecreeper could just be heard above the din, and a nuthatch too with its staccato rendering of fluty notes.

From my vantage point on a seat in the wood I could see new buds on the tips of twigs high in the canopy beautifully silhouetted against the lightening sky. Somewhere up there a chiffchaff called incessantly. The ringing laugh of a green woodpecker momentarily drowned other calls. By now it was after half past five and light enough to see through the trees. An early morning dog-walker appeared silently along the path, his dog scampering on the scent of foxes. Jays gave warning, but the chorus continued unabated. Now the mellow cooing of woodpigeons and mournful call of stockdoves could be heard. A kestrel drifted silently over the treetops and from a distant part of the wood came the high-pitched trill of a lesser spotted woodpecker. Just before six o'clock starlings suddenly appeared, singing lustily with quivering wings, vigorously making up for their earlier absence. With their arrival the sounds of other birds gradually waned. The performance was over.

*Bracket fungus on beech hanger on Salt Box Down.*

Out of the wood it was broad daylight, and only a few minutes' walk to Highgate tube station, where early commuters were already heading for their trains.

Queen's Wood is one of London's ancient habitats. It is very likely that there has been some kind of woodland here ever since prehistoric times. Natural forests of lime and oak, mixed with alder, ash, elm, birch and hazel, were cleared in some of the drier ground in the area of present-day London as long ago as 3000 BC. But on the wetter claylands much of the forest remained until Saxon times. Woods were gradually turned to farmland or, where there were sandy soils, to open heath. Those which remained were not left in their natural state but exploited over many centuries as a source of all manner of woodland products essential to local communities.

Many woods in the countryside around London were recorded in the Domesday Book. Entries included 'wood for 1,450 swine' in the manor of Fulham and 'wood for 100 swine' in Westminster. The county of Middlesex alone contained sufficient woodland for 20,000 swine. To qualify for registration, these woods would have to have had some value and be liable for taxes. No longer natural woodland, they were clearly being utilised by man, probably as coppices cut for timber or as some kind of woodland pasture. It is quite possible that they had been exploited in this way for a considerable time before the Domesday records were taken; in some parts of England traditional uses of woodlands date from the Iron Age.

Opposite *Carpets of wood anemones in Lesnes Abbey Woods.*

Extensive tracts of forest are known to have existed to the north and south of London in medieval times. A twelfth-century account mentions red deer, wild boar and even wild bulls being found in the forest. When John Roque produced his map of London in the late eighteenth century, woodland still blanketed the low ridge of hills north of Croydon as far as Honor Oak and Brockley. This area was known as the Great North Wood, to which Woodside, Norwood and Forest Hill all owe their names. Most of the wood has long since gone but fragments remain around Sydenham Hill and Dulwich. In Roque's time Epping Forest was more extensive too, the lower forest of wood pasture covering what is now Wanstead Flats.

*Coppicing at Oxleas Wood near Greenwich.*

One of the largest woods close to London at that time was Tottenham Wood, which covered nearly 400 acres on the hill now occupied by Alexandra Palace. Towards the end of the century it was cleared, but many other fragments of old woodland persisted well into the nineteenth century. The past hundred years has seen the greatest changes affecting these woodlands, for two reasons. Many disappeared under bricks and mortar as London expanded; Bishop's Wood, just west of Highgate, for example, for which historical records go back to the thirteenth century, was cleared to make way for housing and a golf course in the 1920s. Most of the woods that survived, including Queen's Wood at Highgate, underwent considerable changes because traditional management such as coppicing had ceased.

Coppicing provided a regular supply of timber over the years while avoiding the need to fell a wood and plant new trees. Hazel and other small trees were cut just above the ground, leaving the base of the trunk and roots undisturbed to form a coppice stool from which new stems would sprout. Blocks of hazel coppice were felled on a rotational basis, each block being allowed to grow for about ten years. With sufficient segments in a wood, a continuous supply of timber was assured. Hazel was put to a great variety of uses: long straight branches made good hop poles and posts; it was also used for crates, baskets, hurdles, hoops and stakes. The brushwood was bundled into faggots for firewood or to produce charcoal. In many of these coppice woods, some of the oaks were allowed to grow into mature trees known as 'standards', producing a two-layered effect. These mature trees were needed to provide larger timber for buildings, and also in London for river defences.

Other woods were managed in a very different way as wood pasture, where livestock grazed beneath the trees. Here it was common practice to cut the trees about seven to ten feet above the ground so that the new growth was out of reach of grazing animals. This was known as pollarding; woods of pollarded hornbeam mixed with mature oak were particularly common around the north side of London. As with coppice woods, a timber crop was taken regularly from the pollards, the gnarled old trunks of which might grow for several hundred years. As well as being in considerable demand for firewood, timber of the hornbeam, being very hard, was used for making wagon wheels and agricultural machinery; some say that this tree owes its name to its use for cattle yolks.

The demand for traditional woodland products started to decline early last century, when coal took the place of wood as a fuel and substitutes were found for wood in many developing industries. It soon became uneconomic to continue cutting the trees, so in most cases they were left to grow. After 150 years of neglect, most of the ancient coppice woods in London are now very different from what they used to be. Pollarded hornbeams gradually turned into full-grown trees on ancient trunks. Spindly growths of hazel became mature trees too. Even the oaks grew in stature, and open glades disappeared under continuous canopies. There were other changes too. During this century many woods within the boundary of the built-up area of London have taken on a new role as public open space. Some are now nothing more than parks, and their woodland history is in danger of being forgotten.

Ancient woods surviving to the present day provide a remarkable link with the past. Three hundred years ago Queen's Wood was called Sow Wood Fall or, alternatively, Old Fall. Not far to the north is Coldfall Wood in Finchley. The names imply that these were coppice woodlands, 'fall' being a long established word for an area of coppice cut at one go. It seems that in this case each wood was cut in entirety instead of being divided into smaller blocks. An historical account of the woodlands of Hornsey (by Silvertown in the *London Naturalist* of 1978) suggests that, in the sixteenth century, 'coppicing was rotated between several of the falls of Hornsey and Finchley in order to provide a large constant supply of fuel' to London.

Some of these coppice woods were associated with common land or waste which was grazed by livestock. Banks with hedges around the woods prevented animals from getting into the coppices, where they would easily destroy the young shoots. An ancient wood bank can still be seen in the west of Queen's Wood now marked by a line of pollarded hornbeams. This once formed the boundary between Old Fall and Sow Wood Common. Similar banks survive on the west side of Coldfall Wood, where they once protected the wood from animals grazing Finchley Common.

The variety of plants and insects in ancient woods far exceeds that of more recent woodlands. Many woodland flowers and hundreds of different kinds of insects have survived in these woods only because suitable conditions were perpetuated over many centuries. Once destroyed, this rich assortment of wildlife cannot be restored. Many attractive woodland flowers, such as wood anemone, yellow archangel, wood sorrel and sanicle, are virtually confined to ancient woods. If you find these in your local wood, you can be almost certain that the wood has been there for hundreds of years. Other clues are the presence of field maple, midland hawthorn and wild service tree. Ancient woods sometimes contain very old trees which provide special habitats for certain birds and insects. Woodpeckers and other birds which nest in holes benefit particularly from such old trees, but there are also many species of beetles and some rather specialised flies which spend part of their life-cycle in dead and dying wood. These insects cannot exist in any other habitat and some of them are now becoming extremely rare as really old trees become scarce.

A surprising number of ancient woods can be found in Greater London. In 1984 a survey by the Nature Conservancy Council revealed nearly 200 such woods larger than five acres, totalling about 6500 acres. These woods are scattered through the outer suburbs, with particular concentrations in Bromley, Waltham Forest and Hillingdon. The tree species they contain vary from place to place depending on local soil conditions. Oak and hornbeam woods are commonest on the claylands, alder woods in some of the valleys, and beech hangers on the chalk downs of the south. Each has its own particular selection of wildlife.

A huge cattlegrid by the roundabout on the North Circular road in Woodford is a tangible reminder that this is still part of Epping Forest. Several large woods of ancient oaks and pollarded hornbeams in this area are the remaining fragments of Waltham Forest. A little further north at Buckhurst Hill is an unusual piece of old woodland known as Lord's Bushes and Knighton Wood, where moribund oaks dating from Tudor times stand between patches of younger trees. Many years ago part of this wood was turned into a garden which has since reverted to the wild, creating a beautiful spot with ponds full of waterlilies and yellow flag set among the ancient trees. Other vestiges of Epping Forest along the headwaters of the Ching Brook have magnificent spreading oaks in an open park landscape which was probably much the same when the beautiful timbered building known as Queen Elizabeth's Hunting Lodge was built nearby.

A few miles to the east, straddling the Essex border, is Hainault Forest, which must surely be one of the strangest and yet most beautiful woods in London. It was once part of the Royal Forest of Essex and in 1774 it extended to nearly 5000 acres. Most was cleared in the middle of last century but fortunately about 800 acres survived and the wood was designated as a public open space by special Act of Parliament in 1903. It is a magnificent hornbeam wood in which the ancient pollards, uncut for many decades, have grown into mature trees. But what extraordinary, contorted trees they are: their gnarled and twisted trunks, full of holes and covered in a rash of lumps and bumps where branches were severed long ago, produce an eerie effect.

*Pollarded hornbeams create an eerie feeling in Hainault Forest where the lack of woodland flowers may be due to dense shade and long history of use for wood pasture.* David Goode

By the small carpark in the wood opposite the Camelot public house at Lambourne End is an old iron cattle pound erected in 1904 for enclosing stray cattle in the forest. It must have been odd to see cattle grazing under the hornbeams, but no doubt the forest was used as pasture when the pollards were kept open. Nowadays the old trees provide nest holes for kestrels, stock doves, tawny owls and starlings. The wood is also favoured by hawfinches, one of the most elusive of birds, which may at times be seen feeding on hornbeam fruits. Another speciality of Hainault is the nightingale. During May its song can often be heard from the hawthorn bushes along the south side of the wood. Here there are several strategically placed seats ideal for savouring the song of a nightingale in the early morning sunshine.

◆

South of the Thames, Lesnes Abbey Woods are famous for the finest display of wild daffodils in London. Only a few minutes walk from Abbey Wood station, the area is spectacular in spring. The daffodils are usually at their best by the beginning of April. A few weeks later clumps of wood anemones steal the show, and by May the same woods are full of bluebells. There is also a wealth of birds to be found here. One April day while a pied woodpecker was drumming to announce its territory, I heard a lesser spotted woodpecker trill from the tops of the sweet chestnut trees and, within minutes, the strident call of a green woodpecker. Later that morning I witnessed the spectacular courtship chase of a pair of pied woodpeckers, flying in and out between the trees at great speed, in strong contrast to their normal lazy flight; occasionally they produced a long trilling song. Chiffchaffs sang from the tops of the oak trees and willow warblers could be heard in the birches near the abbey ruins.

*Wild daffodils in Lesnes Abbey Woods near Thamesmead; one of London's finest wild-life spectacles.* David Goode

Opposite *Jack Wood near Shooter's Hill, part of London's ancient oak woodland.*

Paths through Lesnes Abbey Woods are fenced to protect the spring flowers, producing a less natural woodland than would be ideal but one which is nevertheless very beautiful. Many woods elsewhere in London have lost their woodland flowers simply because of the number of people walking through them every day. If there are no well-defined paths, the vegetation of town woodlands does not stand much of a chance.

A few miles further into London another group of ancient woods lies south of Shooters Hill in Greenwich. Oxleas, Jack Wood and Shepherdleas are long-established woods of oak, hazel, ash and hornbeam, parts of which are still actively coppiced. Among the many different woodland plants are about 30 species associated

with ancient woodland. Attractive patches of yellow archangel and wood violet occur, and the more unusual plants include butcher's broom, which is now quite scarce in London. Wild service trees grow in these woods, and the mixture of shrubs and trees includes aspen, wild cherry and guelder rose. A recent census of birds in Oxleas Wood recorded several pairs of nuthatches and treecreepers as well as woodpeckers and spotted flycatchers. More surprising was the presence of wood warblers so far into London. Oxleas is a fine piece of woodland, but its future is currently in the balance; a proposed road scheme through east London would cut right across it.

*Parasol mushrooms in Jack Wood.*

*Opposite King's Wood in Croydon is one of London's most beautiful oak woods with spectacular displays of bluebells in the woodland glades.* David Goode

Even further into London are fragments of ancient oak and hornbeam woods at Dulwich and Sydenham Hill. They also contain many of the flowers typical of long-established woodlands, including in this case solomon's seal and wood sorrel. Despite their location, these woods have a rich birdlife, including woodpeckers and owls; it is even possible to hear cuckoos. Hedgehogs, bank voles and wood mice are all abundant. These must be some of the richest wild habitats near to the centre of London, for it is only six miles from here to St Paul's. Apart from fragments of the Great North Wood which are in the grounds of Dulwich College, it seems that most of these woods have survived only because they lie on slopes which cannot easily be developed. The remnants bear witness to the woodland history of this part of London, particularly the charcoal-burning industry, which is perpetuated locally in names such as Woodhouse, Forresters, Woodman and Burnt Ash. There is hope that the woods themselves will now survive as both Dulwich Upper Wood and Sydenham Hill Wood have recently been designated as nature reserves.

◆

Selsdon Wood on the southern fringe of London recently celebrated 50 years as a nature reserve. It includes 200 acres of oak woodland and old fields with overgrown hedgerows, which were bought by public subscription as a bird sanctuary in 1927. The reserve was officially opened in 1936, when it became the property of the National Trust, and is managed by the London Borough of Croydon. For many years it was regarded simply as a bird sanctuary and managed accordingly. Forestry operations took little account of its value as an ancient oak wood; parts were even felled and replanted with larch and spruce. In the interests of birds there was also vigorous control of pests. A report in 1978 by Jack Penry-Jones stated that pest control required constant attention and went on to list 77 foxes, 786 squirrels and 160 jays killed in the wood between 1973 and 1977! I can understand the need to control squirrels if they are damaging trees, but I find it difficult to accept the killing of foxes or jays in a woodland nature reserve. It is to be hoped that more enlightened attitudes now prevail.

Selsdon Wood is a fine piece of oak woodland with carpets of bluebells and wood anemones and plenty of woodpeckers. Hole-nesting birds have a wide range of nest sites to choose from for there are hundreds of nest boxes among the trees; they come in all shapes and sizes, suitable for everything from a blue tit to a tawny owl or kestrel. The wood is well worth a visit in April or May when the flowers are at their best. Recently, coppicing has been reinstated in places and no doubt the flora will gradually improve as traditonal management is extended to other parts of the wood.

Close by is King's Wood, one of the most beautiful woods in London. It is full of magnificent oaks with attractive woodland glades covered in springtime carpets of bluebells. One morning in May I counted the songs or calls of 25 different sorts of birds in the space of half an hour's walk. One was a wood warbler, whose 'sibilous shivering note' was so aptly described by Gilbert White in the beech hangers of Selborne. There are few places in the London area where this bird can be heard today. Because of its large size King's Wood gives the impression of wildness and it is no surprise to come across a badger set, or to see a fox crossing one of the woodland rides in the evening.

The borough of Bromley is well endowed with woodland, with numerous beech hangers on the downs south of Orpington and several large oak woods in the outer suburbs between Orpington and Bromley. Petts Wood, a large National Trust woodland, is probably the best known. It has a mixture of oak, birch and alder and is one of the few places where lily of the valley still grows. An old woodland bank with a line of pollarded oaks marks the boundary between the wood and the old common. Several of the woods between Bromley and Keston are still actively coppiced. One of these consists largely of coppiced alder trees, which present a most unusual sight. Nearby is Woodcock Grove, which is said to be a haunt of the woodcock even today.

The most extraordinary wood in Bromley must be Park Wood at Scadbury. Until very recently this was part of a private estate and is now being managed as a nature reserve by the borough. When I visited this wood before there was public access, it felt totally isolated from the surrounding suburbs of Chislehurst and Sidcup. This impression was heightened by the presence of a pair of cottages in the middle of the wood, with a cluster of beehives under the trees and stacks of firewood by the back door. The sight was like something out of the New Forest. Close by were ancient oaks and beeches. Some were dead but remained standing, their spreading branches gaunt amid the new growth of sycamores. Others were reduced to no more than hollow trunks with the stumps of former branches; like sentinels standing guard over the wood, they gave the place an eerie feeling. Yet others retained life in their limbs but were nonetheless full of holes and rotten wood. You could walk inside some of them and look up through the hollow trunk to the sky. The rings were still visible on one tree which had been felled years ago and a careful count revealed that it was nearly 400 years old. These trees are the remnants of park woodland dating from the time of Elizabeth I.

---

*Opposite Park Wood at Scadbury near Chislehurst. Dead and dying oaks dating from an Elizabethan hunting forest now harbour a host of specialised insects and hole-nesting birds. The ancient trees are surrounded by recent growths of sycamore.*

This wood has gone through several phases. In Elizabethan times the oaks were broad, spreading trees growing in relatively open conditions, creating a kind of wood pasture in which trees were spaced out from one another as in parts of Epping Forest. Some of these oaks were pollarded before the end of the seventeenth century and beeches were planted among them, some of which have grown to a considerable size. A second phase was the planting of large numbers of oaks, including some turkey oaks, around the beginning of the nineteenth century. Some of the turkey oaks near Perry Street Shaw on the northern edge of the wood could well date from even earlier; they must be some of the oldest turkey oaks in Britain. But the woods also contain many other species, including rowan, birch, alder, maple, yew and, unfortunately, sycamore. During the past 40 years there has been little active management of the woods and sycamore has spread into many areas. Its bright-green stems contrast sharply with the trunks of oak and beech and it will present something of a problem to those who manage these woods in the future.

Not surprisingly Scadbury Park is a marvellous place for woodland birds. As well as kestrels, owls and woodpeckers, there are ring-necked parakeets. It seems that several pairs of the latter nest in this wood; their shrill calls are a familiar sound in early spring.

Another woodland curiosity of much greater antiquity can be seen at Spring Park on the borders of Bromley and Croydon near Addington. The borough boundary runs through the wood, where it is marked by an ancient wood bank dividing Spring Park from the delightfully named Threehalfpenny Wood. Here is a small area of lime wood which, so far as I know, is the only example of its kind in London. The trees are small-leaved limes, the same species that grew in the original forest covering the landscape in prehistoric times. Nowadays it is relatively scarce as a woodland tree but at Spring Park there is a row of ancient pollarded limes growing along the line of the old wood bank, where the path strikes up the hill by the Croydon boundary sign.

Perivale Wood by the Grand Union Canal in west London is another remarkable survivor. This wood owes its continued existence to the far-sighted action of the Brent Valley branch of the Selborne Society, who first suggested that it should be protected as a wildlife sanctuary. That was in 1902! They appointed a keeper to look after it in 1905 and the wood was bought by the society in 1922. Even in 1927 it was still surrounded by open countryside and was being managed as coppice woodland. Ten years later the London suburbs spread around it and, had it not already been protected, it is unlikely that it would have survived. In 1974 Perivale Wood was designated as an official Local Nature Reserve by the Borough of Ealing.

Although it is hemmed in on one side by industry, the wood retains all its natural characteristics. It has not suffered the fate of so many other woodlands caught up in urban areas which have gradually lost their woodland flowers. This wood is a genuine piece of the original country now in town. It is famous for its bluebells and is open to the public on the first Sunday in May, when most flowers are at their best. The wood has been intensively studied and is carefully managed to encourage a rich variety of birds, plants and insects typical of ancient oak and hazel coppice woods.

One of the most extensive and finest areas of ancient woodland in London lies on the very edge of the metropolis between Ruislip and Northwood. Ruislip Woods are made up of four large woods which together cover 550 acres. A park for wild beasts of the forest was recorded here in the Domesday Book and the ancient earth bank which once enclosed this park can still be seen in Park Wood. Nearby in Mad Bess Wood are numerous earthworks, relics of a complex history of coppicing since medieval times. These woods have long been of great importance to the local economy. They supplied timber for the Tower of London and the Palace of Westminster in the fourteenth century. Records of a well-established trade in woodland products indicate continuous use over many centuries. Thirty men were working in Park Wood in the eighteenth century; and it is said that by 1880 women and children were able to make more money selling firewood to the London markets from this area than their menfolk could make on the local farms.

All these woods are mixtures of oak and hornbeam. Some have quantities of alder, aspen and even beech, providing unusual variety and a strong sense of the ancient wildwood. There is an attractive woodland flora too, especially in Park Wood and Copse Wood, which offer a wide choice of wet and dry conditions. Wood anemone, betony, cow wheat and goldilocks are typical of the variety; so too are the 500 or so different kinds of fungi that can be found here. Badgers can occasionally be seen and sparrowhawks hunt along the woodland rides. In winter the woods are frequented by flocks of redpolls and siskins, and as in other hornbeam woods their larger relative the hawfinch may sometimes be spotted. But of all the woodland birds at Ruislip my favourite is the woodcock. No longer shot for sport, it still nests here in small numbers, and at dusk in spring when birds are out 'roding' you may hear the 'whisp' of a woodcock coming through the gloom, and if lucky you may catch a strange grunting call as one of the birds passes overhead during its ceremonial 'beating of the bounds'.

The value of Ruislip Woods for wildlife was officially recognised in 1950, when the Nature Conservancy designated them a Site of Special Scientific Interest, but their significance is even greater now, as many examples of oak and hornbeam wood elsewhere have been destroyed. One of the woods at Ruislip, Bayhurst, is now a country park with barbecue, picnic sites and a developing woodland craft centre. It caters for recreational needs; but the other woods have merit enough between them to be regarded as a nature reserve of national quality, one of the few places in London to warrant that distinction.

Like the woodcock on its evening flight, we come full circle on our excursion round the London woods to our starting point on Highgate Hill. Here we can look again at the town woods along Muswell Hill Road. We are fortunate indeed that Queen's and Highgate Woods have survived in such a situation. They obviously give great pleasure to many people, but I suspect it goes deeper than that. Trees and woods have a special place in the human psyche. Our emotional attachment to the wildwood has long-established roots and it is no surprise that the woods at Highgate are greatly loved by those who know them well. For town dwellers they have a special role – not just as a link with the wild but as a means of gaining spiritual refreshment. For many they are the 'mountains and wilderness' of the city which can be savoured every day. If there is a yearning for green within us, nowhere is it to be met more readily than in a wood.

Given the pressures of modern city life, it is a miracle that Highgate's woods remain so intact. Magnificent oaks and hornbeams abound and many ancient features have managed to survive. The variety of birds is steadily increasing. Green woodpeckers, infrequent visitors only a few years ago, are now well established. Spotted flycatchers nest by an entrance to Highgate Wood, and recently one of the keepers even had hawfinches visiting the birdbath in his cottage garden by the Archway Road. Speckled wood butterflies are seen at times and there are wood mice and field voles in these woods, as well as foxes living on the old railway bank nearby.

However, in other ways, city life has taken its toll on the wildness of these woods, especially in the case of flowers. The effect is less pronounced in Queen's Wood, which retains some of its woodland flowers, especially in the damper parts beside the stream, where patches of wood anemone, sorrel and celandine still occur among the trees. Elsewhere woodland flowers are few and far between. Highgate Wood has fared less well. Where there is green underfoot, it is well-worn grass, and much of the ground between the trees has been trampled bare over the years.

*Fly agaric toadstools on a woodland bank near the Thames in Woolwich.*

Before the turn of the century Highgate Woods were a blaze of colour each spring with swathes of bluebells and thousands of wood anemones. Few are to be seen now. These glories of ancient woodland have long since gone, ousted by the sheer number of people and an urge for tidiness among those who have for many years managed the wood as if it were a town park. It is now a hundred years since the City of London Corporation took responsibility for the wood, but even in the 1890s there were complaints about its beauty and wildness being destroyed by thinning of the undergrowth. A. E. Housman wrote an amusing letter to the London *Standard* in 1894 drawing attention to the redbrick houses, and scarlet petticoats on washing lines, which had become visible from the very centre of the wood. Problems of a different kind were reported by the London Natural History Society in 1968, when planting of exotic conifers stimulated the society to recommend more traditional planting of oak and hornbeam.

Times are changing. A new wind is blowing through the trees. One of the Highgate keepers has recently been busy planting woodland flowers. Wild garlic, red campion, dog's mercury, stitchwort, honeysuckle, violets and foxgloves: all have been planted in recent years. Maybe bluebells and wood anemones will follow. New efforts are being made to encourage underscrub for warblers. To be really effective, parts would need to be set aside for coppicing and to encourage natural regeneration. It will take time and a concerted effort, but the trend is being reversed; the former glory of this wildwood may yet be restored on Highgate Hill.

# ◆ MEADOWS AND HEDGEROWS ◆

HANGING on a friend's wall is a beautiful early seventeenth-century map depicting a small piece of English countryside. It shows a patchwork of fields and woods with streams, lanes and village greens. Tiny red-roofed cottages and turreted churches are drawn in their appropriate places and each field is coloured according to its ownership. The fields are inscribed with a host of fascinating names, each one a clue to the history of this area: Lord's Meade, Peartree Feild, Crow Nest, Great Gallow Fielde, Mill Meade, Home Pasture, The Slype, Broad Waters, Parsonage Grounds, Butchers Feilde, Downehills, Clay Hangers and The Wilde Marshe. Not only are the fields named individually, but their tenants are included too. So Rose Feilds are attributed to Widow Pearson, the Woodridings to Mrs Candler, Crow Nest to Thos Swyner, and Great Snares Mead to Edward Barkham.

But where is this particular piece of countryside? It could be almost anywhere in the claylands of southern England, which covered large parts of the old county of Middlesex. Glancing over the map one day, I suddenly realised that the Wilde Marshe lay alongside the River Lea, and it wasn't long before I picked out Wood Greene and Stamford Hill. It is in fact a map of part of the parishes of Tottenham and Edmonton, in what is now an almost totally built-up district of north London between Alexandra Palace and the River Lea.

This detailed map of rural Tottenham was produced by Thomas Clay in 1619, but it isn't necessary to delve that far back to see how the countryside around London used to look. Rocque's map of 1769 and the first ordnance survey maps early last century show that virtually the whole of the clayland of Middlesex used to be covered by a tapestry of small fields and hedgerows interspersed with occasional blocks of the original woodland.

Graphic descriptions of the wildlife that inhabited the clayland are available too. When Richard Jefferies moved from Wiltshire to Surbiton in 1877, Surbiton was nothing more than a village on the very edge of London. From his home in Ewell Road

– now surrounded by the built-up areas of Kingston and Tolworth – he explored the nearby countryside along the Hogsmill River and around Old Maldon. There he found green lanes and field paths, hayfields and hedgerows and a copse not far from his house where he listened to turtle doves, cuckoos, sedge warblers and nightingales. As he wrote in *Nature Near London* (1883), he was surprised and delighted by the richness of his discoveries:

> Along the roads and lanes the quantity and variety of life in the hedges was really astonishing. Magpies, jays, woodpeckers – both green and pied – kestrels hovering overhead, sparrow-hawks darting over gateways, hares by the clover, weasels on the mounds, stoats at the edge of the corn. I missed but two birds, the corncrake and the grasshopper lark, and found these another season.

From his window in the evening he could hear partridges calling each other to roost, and the nightingales never ceased to amaze him for he had never before heard so many. The blue meadow geranium, or cranesbill, in the nearby fields was another of his delights.

What Jefferies saw around Surbiton was probably fairly typical of the farmland surrounding London at that time. Much of the farming landscape of Middlesex survived until almost the end of the last century, since when the rapid expansion of London engulfed farm after farm. Rural scenes from what are now the suburbs of London are well depicted in Luker's illustrations to Percy Fitzgerald's *London City Suburbs*, published in 1893. His pictures show cows lying in pastures by the church at Leytonstone, horses grazing meadows in lower Sydenham, and flocks of sheep in the meadows at Kingsbury, where pollarded willows grew along the banks of the River Brent. There were hayfields at Friern Barnet and rushy meadows at Perivale, a farmyard in Kilburn and a rutted cart track beneath an avenue of elms in Acton. Even Daisy Lane in Fulham still had tangled hedgerows and a five-bar gate leading into the nearby fields. Below Muswell Hill was a patchwork of fields, and the rough grassland of the hill itself was covered in wild flowers. Everywhere, it seems, there were elm trees along the hedgerows.

Fitzgerald was well aware that huge tracts of London's countryside had already disappeared under bricks and mortar during Victoria's reign, and that many of the scenes depicted in his book would soon meet the same fate. The very countryside of Richard Jefferies was soon to disappear. Not long after he left Surbiton in 1882 the village was gradually overtaken by London. By 1908, when Edward Thomas visited Ewell Road, in the course of writing a biography of Jefferies, Surbiton had already become part of the metropolis. Such was the speed of progress that Ewell Road now had electric trams running down to Tolworth. Thomas's description of Tolworth Farm just a little way beyond the tramway terminus has a familiar ring about it:

> The flat elmy meadows though they retain the scattered houses and ricks of what was once a hamlet have a dejected and demoralised air of defeat by the city.

There are similarities between what Thomas saw and many places on the fringe of London even today. But not far away there were still conical cornricks at Tolworth Court Farm and oak woods with rookeries beyond the Hogsmill River.

Despite London's spread, it remains possible to find vestiges of the original countryside in among the streets and houses of suburbia. In place of former village greens there may be a patch of grass carefully protected as part of the village common. Acton Green and Turnham Green may not be traditional village greens with duck ponds, but at least they still have their grass. Wood Green boasts its village common too, but there is not much grass left at nearby West Green in Tottenham. Others, such as Kensal Green and Willesden Green, retain only their names.

Sometimes there are more tangible reminders of London's rural heritage. In the 1930s suburb of Eastcote near Ruislip are several farm buildings dating from the sixteenth and seventeenth centuries. Like so many other 'listed' buildings dotted around suburbia, the Old Barn House and Field End Farm now make attractive homes or offices. Not far away at Headstone near Harrow an ancient wooden tithe barn and moated manor house stand by the local recreation ground surrounded by ordinary suburban streets. The antiquity of such buildings is appreciated and they will be protected.

Many of the more natural features in the countryside have also managed to survive, sometimes in the oddest places. In the same residential area of Eastcote, oaks of remarkable age and stature, remnants of former parkland, stand between the modern houses. Such ancient oaks seem incongruous, yet they have much to say about the history of this place. Similar trees in the suburbs of Wanstead and Whipps Cross indicate the previous southerly extent of the wood pasture of Epping Forest. In some localities the last vestige of a village green, or patch of common land, may be detected by the presence of gnarled and twisted old hawthorn trees growing on what is nowadays just another patch of roadside grass. A good example can be seen about a mile south of Wallington, where a group of such hawthorns make a magnificent spectacle in May.

A surprising number of old hedgerows have also survived in twentieth-century housing and industrial estates. They are easy to spot because they tend to be very overgrown with hawthorn bushes now becoming small trees. Such hedges can even be seen in Brixton among high-rise flats along King's Avenue not far from the South Circular Road. Bushy hedges of this kind tend to be commoner in the outer suburbs, where they form a notable feature along some of the roadsides. North of Romford, where the A12 trunk road passes through the suburbs of Harold Hill and Collier Row, there are some magnificent stretches of old hedges, especially along the line of the former Roman road. In one section a dual carriageway has been constructed on either side of the ancient hedge line, leaving the overgrown hedge complete with swathes of cow parsley along the central reservation. A little further west beyond Gallows Corner this busy road is fringed with hawthorn hedges for a considerable distance. When the may is in blossom, it is strange to see it illuminated under the continuous belt of arc lamps.

Some rural enclaves are now totally surrounded by built-up areas. Older residents of Wembley have seen Barn Hill and Horsenden Hill become islands of countryside within the continuous sea of housing in north-west London. Scadbury Park near Chislehurst is another example, a microcosm of traditional Kentish countryside encapsulated within the suburbs of Sidcup. In other places, fingers of open land extend into urban districts from the countryside surrounding London. On the south side of the city a wedge of open countryside protrudes well in to the suburbs of Croydon and Bromley. Similar enclaves occur between Chigwell and Romford in the north-east and at Totteridge just north of Finchley. There is another large expanse of open countryside around Harefield between Northwood and the Colne Valley.

Above *Buttercup fields and May blossom at Brook Farm Open Space along the Dollis Brook between Totteridge and Barnet.* David Goode

*A tangle of ladies bedstraw and tufted vetch on Ham Lands.* David Goode

These large tracts of countryside have remained intact because the land was bought by public authorities to prevent the further spread of London. During the 1930s Middlesex County Council purchased 10,000 acres of farmland around the edge of the city, thereby creating the beginnings of London's green belt. Such areas have been protected ever since, though it was not until the mid-1950s that green-belt planning was formally introduced. The present boundary of the built-up area is very much controlled by the designation of surrounding areas of open countryside as green-belt land. For the past 30 years London's green belt has had a pronounced effect in constraining further expansion of the suburbs; without it, further growth would have been inevitable, and it is most unlikely that any of the large enclaves of countryside now remaining in Greater London would have survived.

Many of the surviving areas of open land have all the traditional features of original farmland. There are hay fields, rough pasture, 'field' ponds, ditches, spinneys and copses, old footpaths and miles of overgrown hedgerows separating the small fields. Perhaps because of the situation of such places close to the urban fringe, the pressure for agricultural improvement there has not been so great as in more intensively managed farmland elsewhere in lowland England, where such features have now largely disappeared. Because of the widespread nature of recent changes in the English landscape, some of the remnants of farmland in London's countryside now have a rarity value which is only just becoming appreciated.

In some cases open land is farmed successfully right up to the boundary of suburbia, as at Selsdon and New Addington near Croydon. But farming on the edge of the metropolis has its difficulties. Immediate proximity to housing estates can create problems of vandalism, theft and constant trespass, which farmers find it difficult to cope with. Little wonder that they eventually sell out and the land is no longer farmed. Sometimes it is bought by local councils to provide outdoor recreational facilities such as country parks and golf courses. Trent Park and Hainault Country Park are now popular places for weekend visitors. Though on the very edge of the suburbs, they manage to retain a genuine feeling of countryside. At Hainault some of the old farm buildings have been retained, and it is gratifying to see that they continue to attract some of their associated wildlife. In the tops of old stable doors are carefully constructed holes to allow swallows to fly in and out when the buildings are shut. Cut many years ago by a carpenter who obviously enjoyed his work, some even have special little 'doorsteps' at their entrance holes for the birds to perch on. Swallows are still there, nesting on beams above the parks department tractors and mowing machinery. On the other side of London at Harefield in the Colne Valley two working farms are open to the public. Park Lodge Farm has a farm centre used daily by parties of schoolchildren, and there are guided trails at Knightscote farm nearby. In 1985 a pair of barn owls was reintroduced to Highway Farm at Park Lodge. They nested successfully, producing several young, and it is hoped that they will form the nucleus of a renewed population of these beautiful white owls.

In many places farmland survives although it is no longer actively farmed, creating neglected areas of no-man's-land between town and real countryside. All around the fringes of London you cannot miss the hawthorn hedges rapidly turning to scrub, thistle-filled fields grazed by a few ponies, unmanaged copses with trees covered in ivy, ponds full of old cars, mattresses and refrigerators. Such sure signs of abandoned farmland must be very familiar to speculative builders who regard such areas as ripe only for development.

The wildlife of this abandoned farmland on the edge of the countryside can be remarkably rich. Admittedly, you won't find many meadow flowers left in the heavily grazed pony paddocks; in that sense, these areas of 'horsey culture' leave a lot to be desired. But the overgrown hedges and old hedgerow trees are ideal spots for a variety of birds. Tree sparrows, little owls and stock doves can all be found nesting in holes in hedgerow trees, and the hedges are popular with long-tailed tits, yellowhammers, linnets, lesser whitethroats and even turtle doves. They are good places for butterflies too, with speckled wood, small copper, wall and comma frequently encountered. Fine examples of such hedgerows can be seen from the footpaths across the fields a mile or two south of the centre of Bromley. Others grace the buttercup fields next to the high-rise flats of Slade Green near Erith. North of the river a patchwork of old hedgerows enlivens the otherwise bleak landscape on the fringe of Hornchurch and Upminster; while, on the other side of London, similar old hedges surround pony paddocks near Oaks Park in the countryside fringe of Carshalton. Indeed, if you take a walk in the first stretch of countryside you come to almost anywhere around the edge of the capital, you are bound to find something of this kind.

Remnants of old farmland can also be found closer to central London. A mile or so east of the centre of Croydon is Lloyd Park, where some of the fields and hedges of Coombe Farm survive. In summer swallows can be seen hawking over these fields. They nest in outbuildings of the nearby golf-club house, which makes a suitable alternative to traditional farm buildings. More surprising are Downham Fields in Lewisham, only eight miles from Charing Cross. Although totally surrounded by housing and now regarded simply as a recreation ground, these fields contain a variety of meadow plants which have endured from farming times. Bird's-foot trefoil, cat's ear, goat's beard, smooth hawksbeard, agrimony and hardheads can all be found growing in the rougher parts of this patch of suburban grassland. Another vestige of old pasture can be seen by the Edgware Road where it crosses the Silk Stream at the Hyde near Hendon court house. Yarrow and hardheads still flower in this tiny patch of rough grassland by the stream. It is often used for grazing ponies, an unexpected sight along this busy road. The equivalent meadow on the north bank of the stream is more in keeping with the times: it is occupied by a supermarket.

As long as the traditional management has been continued over the years, even small pockets of meadowland may play host to a remarkable variety of plants. One such place, which became known to botanists as recently as 1984, is a patch of hay meadow by the Yeading Brook in Hillingdon, where a number of rare plants survive. The meadow, which is owned by Hillingdon Council, is regularly cut for hay and has apparently never been improved. One of the notable plants still growing there is the pepper saxifrage, a close relative of fennel, which is gradually disappearing from many parts of England as old meadows are ploughed up or reseeded to create more productive grassland. But it is in Hare's Hollows that the most interesting plants have survived. These are two small wet hollows in the meadows which owe their name not to the mad March hare, but to the botanical enthusiast who discovered them. These apparently insignificant depressions are full of fascinating plants. Here, in addition to patches of delightful crimson-flowered grass vetchling and tiny adder's-tongue ferns, there is a substantial colony of an extremely rare plant of the umbellifer tribe known as the narrow-leafed water dropwort. This was last recorded in Middlesex in 1815, when it was found growing in Marylebone Fields; no doubt the meadows there provided a similar wet habitat at that time, but they have long since been replaced by Regent's Park.

Another former ancient meadow is Ham Lands, which lies within a great loop of the Thames opposite Twickenham. Early last century it was marked on maps as Ham Field. At that time it was mostly an open expanse of riverside pasture which flooded only too readily when the river was in spate. The word 'ham' has long been used when referring to meadows within the knee-bend of a river. Indeed, riverside pastures along the Severn in Worcestershire are known locally as 'hams' and have a long tradition as common grazing. It is possible that both Ham Lands and the nearby meadows, which were once known simply as Petersham, owe their names to this same traditional use. The meadows at Petersham are still cut for hay and in places you can find patches of the beautiful blue meadow cranesbill, of which Richard Jefferies was so fond.

Ham Lands itself is now very different from what it once was. In postwar years a large section of it was excavated for gravel, and part of one of the flooded gravel pits remains, now used as a marina. Over most of the area the pits were filled and the land has gradually reverted to a more natural character. Now it is a wild and bushy place where patches of rough meadowland form flower-filled enclaves in the fast-encroaching scrub. Despite all the changes it has undergone, Ham Lands remains a wonderful contrast to the suburbs across the river. You only have to cross the footbridge from Teddington near the weir and strike off along any one of the many footpaths across the Ham to find yourself in a different world. It has so wild a feel about it that it is difficult to believe that you are in London. I can well understand how people get lost here. It is easy to become disorientated and find yourself back at the riverbank just when you thought you were reaching the other side, particularly if your attention has been distracted by the remarkable variety of wild flowers.

By the end of July tall stems of cocksfoot and Yorkshire fog in the rough grassland are mixed with an abundance of colourful meadow flowers. The ground is covered in clumps of bright yellow ladies bedstraw, tiny heads of black medic, pink cups of the delicately marked field bindweed and yellow flowers of creeping cinquefoil. Clovers and vetches occur in profusion, including the attractive purple flowers of our native tufted vetch often mixed with the pale lilac of goat's rue, a native of southern Europe now well established in Britain. Cut-leafed cranesbill and yarrow grow among taller flowers of meadowsweet, comfrey, hardheads, tansey and hogweed. Here and there are the strange dark red globular flowerheads of crow garlic, a plant which appears to thrive in close proximity to the Thames. In some places bee orchids and even pyramidal orchids can be found, a sure sign that chalky soil was sometimes used to fill the old gravel pits. In fact there are plenty of surprises here for the botanist, for you never know what plant will turn up next.

In the summer these grasslands are full of insects. Redtailed bumblebees gather nectar from the hardheads and wherever you walk there seem to be brown butterflies — skippers and meadow browns by the hundred. Flocks of goldfinches dance from place to place feeding on seedheads, and kestrels drift overhead watching for voles. The meadows have their attractions later in the year too, when frost on the hogweed or tanseyheads produces patterns of great beauty, and snipe fly off into a winter sky from their resting places among the tussocks of frozen grass.

If Ham Lands is difficult to get to by public transport, Horsenden Hill near Wembley presents no problems. The walk from Perivale station on the Central Line to the top of this hill and on to Sudbury Town on the Picadilly Line is little over a mile. It must be one of the finest walks provided by London Transport anywhere in London. Shortly after leaving the station, you pass Perivale Wood nature reserve and then cross the Grand Union Canal. From an entrance in Horsenden Lane a path leads through old pastures to the top of the hill, which at 276 feet provides a spectacular view over the whole of west London and, given a clear day, well beyond.

Horsenden Hill is known to have been occupied by man for at least 7000 years.

Stone Age flint tools have been found here and traces of an Iron Age hill fort can be seen near to the summit. The flanks of the hill have been farmed for many centuries, at one time producing wheat and, more recently, in the nineteenth century, providing hay for London's cab-horses. Within this 250-acre island of countryside in Ealing there are extensive areas of old meadows and unimproved pasture. Like the hay meadows along the Yeading Brook in Hillingdon, these meadows still have flowers such as pepper saxifrage, sneezewort and adder's-tongue fern. In addition burnet saxifrage and ragged robin can also be found. All of these are typical of ancient unimproved grasslands. Similar plants grow in the old pastures of Long Mead and Home Mead on the flanks of the hill, where twelve different kinds of clover and vetch can be found, including grass vetchling, hairy tare, zig-zag clover and dyer's greenweed. This last plant was at one time widely used in the dying of cloth; yellow pigment from it was mixed with the blue pigment from woad, to produce a green dye.

In summer the rough grassland is full of butterflies. Those most often seen include the orange tip, small copper, wall, common blue, meadow brown and three different kinds of skipper. Grayling, marbled white and even grizzled skipper may also be seen on occasions. Many of these are directly dependent on particular plants growing in these fields, either as a food for caterpillars or as a source of nectar for the adult butterflies.

The field pattern of Horsenden Hill is very long established. Hedgerows are much the same now as on the parish map of 1775. It is thought that most are at least 400 or 500 years old. An even older parish boundary hedge forms the present boundary between Horsenden and Sudbury golf courses. Dog's mercury and bluebells occur in some of these hedges along with some 20 different species of native trees and shrubs. In addition to the commoner species there are specimens of Midland hawthorn, field maple, dogwood, hornbeam, wild privet, crab apple and even spindle, the presence of which clearly points to the hedges' great antiquity. (The number of different trees and shrubs in a thirty-yard length of hedge is commonly held to correspond with the number of centuries it has been established.)

It is fortunate indeed that Horsenden Hill survived the rapid spread of suburban housing and light industry which blanketed neighbouring parts of west London during the 1930s. Apparently it was only the difficult ground conditions that prevented it from going the way of all the rest. This island of countryside is now under public ownership and is managed by the London Borough of Ealing in ways that are intended to ensure the survival of its various natural habitats. Hay meadows are now managed in the traditional fashion, a hay crop being taken in July and, when possible, another in September. The old pastures are no longer subjected to the destructive process of mechanical mowing. The borough has even considered the possibility of reintroducing livestock: perhaps we shall see flocks of sheep on them again one day. Hedge laying has already been reintroduced to maintain the hedgerows properly, and areas of scrub invading the meadows are being held in check. The borough has also produced a splendid pamphlet on the natural history of the hill for visitors following the countryside walk. Although the land is no longer farmed, there is now real hope that with all this care and understanding the wildlife of Horsenden Hill will indeed survive.

Similar projects are under way at Barn Hill in Brent, another island of countryside not many miles to the north. Here, in the Fryent Country Park, a hay crop is taken off the meadows each year and hedge laying has been reintroduced. Local volunteers in the

Barn Hill Conservation Group have even organised the replanting of an ancient hedge bank and are busy restoring some of the old farm ponds. A fascinating discovery in one of these ponds in 1984 was a species of midge (*Dixella attica*) previously unknown in the London area and known in only seven other places in Britain. One wonders how many other creatures like this rare midge are still to be discovered in these fragments of rural London.

Outside the Northern Line tube station at Totteridge and Whetstone is a signpost indicating a public footpath to Barnet one and a half miles away. Here you are on the very edge of the suburbs, where a broad swathe of countryside survives between Barnet and Edgware. The path crosses buttercup meadows alongside the meandering Dollis Brook, a headwater of the River Brent. Large hawthorn bushes and magnificent trees of oak, ash, willow and horse-chestnut grow along the banks of the stream. It's an attractive spot in early summer when the may is out and the stream sides are clothed in a lush growth of cow parsley. Linnets and goldfinches call from the hedgerows and you may well see grey wagtails and kingfishers along the brook.

These meadows and hedgerows were once part of Brook Farm. Fields to the west were turned into the South Herts golf course as long ago as 1870, but the meadows bordering the brook itself remained and now form Brook Farm Open Space. A man who has lived here since 1929, whom I met when he was out walking his dog, assured me that the area is exactly as it always used to be. Aware of the hum of countless bees foraging in the treetops and a sea of yellow buttercups covering the meadow, I could well believe him.

At the north end of the meadows the red roofs of Barnet come into view above the tangled hedgerows. Rows and rows of chimney pots and not a bird in sight: what a contrast. From here it is a short walk through suburban streets to the end of the tube line at High Barnet.

Further up the Dollis Brook are Totteridge Fields. Here, in a shallow valley between Totteridge and Barnet, is a remarkable patch of traditional countryside with hayfields full of wild flowers and miles of fine old hedges. A similar area lies between Highwood Hill and Darlands Lake just to the south. Old footpaths can still be found crossing the fields and here you can see what the traditional hay meadows were really like. Some of the flowers are already familiar from Horsenden Hill, but these fields contain a greater variety of species. As any representative of a county wildlife trust knows, many of the flowers growing here have become decidedly scarcer in the English countryside as meadows of this kind have disappeared.

Few of the damp fields around Totteridge have been improved in agricultural terms so there is little of the rye-grass which is so prevalent nowadays. Traditional meadow grasses of cock's foot, bents, crested dog's tail and Yorkshire fog are still the order of the day. Among these grow meadowsweet, ragged robin, and devil's-bit scabious, all of them a sure sign of wet conditions. Great burnet grows here too, a larger relative of the much commoner salad burnet, standing nearly three feet high. Its dark red flowers are much favoured by a great variety of flies and butterflies. Another flower which is plentiful here and very popular with the insects, especially bees, is sneezewort, often growing alongside pepper saxifrage. Every head of sneezewort and yarrow seems to be covered in a host of hover flies and other insects. Less obvious, down between the blades of the grass, are delicate blue harebells and the delightful yellow flowers of meadow vetchling.

Among the blackthorn and may of the hedgerows are crab apples, hazel, hornbeam, maple and even wild service trees. Judging by the number and variety of wayside trees, it seems that these hedgerows must date from at least Elizabethan times. With yellowhammers and whitethroats singing from the hedges and flocks of jackdaws foraging in the fields, it is still a genuinely rural scene.

A few miles further north, near Arkley, one of the few surviving green lanes in London wends its way through the fields between tall bushy hedges. Wild angelica, foxgloves, red campions and hedge woundwort grow in the grassy edges of this ancient track, just as they did nearly 400 years ago when Thomas Clay drew the intricate pattern of green lanes on his map of Tottenham.

# ◆ DOWNLAND ◆

LOOK SOUTH ACROSS London on a clear day from Hampstead or Highgate, and you can see a line of wooded hills on the far horizon, 30 miles away. These are the chalk hills of the North Downs, which form a natural boundary around the southern edge of London. Greater London reaches its highest point (245 metres or 804 feet) on the crest of the downs just north of Westerham.

Between this point and the built-up parts of Bromley and Croydon to the north is the largest stretch of open countryside within the metropolis. It is a high, windswept district of arable farmland and scattered woods, where winter snow lingers along the hedgerows. It is a world apart from the leafy suburbs of Croydon and Orpington just a few miles away. Steep-sided valleys gouged out of the chalk, produce scenery of a special character not found elsewhere in London. Here are remnants of a downland landscape caught between the spreading fingers of suburbia and fragmented by the onslaught of modern agriculture.

In Tudor times you could travel the entire length of the downs across open sheepwalk. In the mid-eighteenth century the excellent flavour of the mutton produced on Banstead Downs was attributed to the quality of the 'pile', or turf, which was composed of English white clover, trefoil and thyme. Countless skylarks sang here and wheatears could be seen by the score. Stone curlews, too, were once a feature of these hills; so numerous were they in southern England during the late eighteenth century that Gilbert White would note their passing every year in April as they flew over Selborne by night. It is a long time since these shy birds nested regularly on the chalkland south of London; the last known occurrence was a pair which nested near Caterham in 1900. Wheatears have gone too, though a few pairs still nested on Banstead Downs even in the 1930s.

During this century the downlands of south London have suffered profound changes. In the areas of open countryside that remain much of the sheep pasture has been ploughed up. In the prevailing economic climate, sheep have given way to arable crops, and nowadays the tops of the downs are yellow with oil seed rape. Some patches of downland survived on slopes that were too steep to plough, but even these have suffered from the changes on surrounding farmland. Because these areas of grassland are small and isolated from one another, local farmers no longer find it profitable to stock them with sheep. So they remain ungrazed and neglected. Since the 1950s, when rabbit numbers were dramatically reduced by myxomatosis, these vestiges of downland have gradually been covered by a tide of hawthorn scrub. Already many have been transformed from open pasture to thorny thickets, and others are rapidly going the same way.

The southward spread of London's suburbs has also had a profound effect. Ribbon development along the valleys of Purley and Whiteleafe, and extensive housing developments on the plateau at Kenley and New Addington, have extended the boundaries of modern London into what was once open downland. Nowadays any area of open land that still exists within these outer suburbs is almost invariably used as a golf course. Though most of the downland itself has gone, names like Purley Downs and Banstead Downs provide a link with the past.

Despite all these pressures, a few fragments of chalk downland have survived.

*Festoons of old man's beard on the chalk hills of south London.*

Farthing Down near Coulsdon was bought by the City of London Corporation in 1877 to save it from destruction and has since been managed 'for the recreation and enjoyment of the public'. The City Corporation also succeeded in protecting another fine piece of chalkland at Riddlesdown in the outskirts of Purley. Had it not been for the City, it is doubtful whether any downland in these outer London suburbs would have been preserved.

Further to the east, in the countryside between New Addington and Biggin Hill, some fine patches of chalk downland have, so far, escaped conversion to arable farmland. Another piece of land, near the village of Downe, is run as a nature reserve by the Kent Trust for Nature Conservation. (It was at Downe Bank that Charles Darwin made many of his observations on wild orchids.) Here you can still find the rich variety of flowers and butterflies which make these downlands so attractive.

One of my favourite spots on the downs is a rather secluded south-facing slope which is covered in a host of chalkland flowers. On a hot summer's day the grassy slopes are alive with the droning of bees and the incessant rasping of grasshoppers. The scent of wild thyme and marjoram fills the air and everywhere one looks there are butterflies and other insects feeding among the flowers.

Leaving the path and climbing the grassy slope, one becomes more acutely aware of the profusion of different plants in the short dry turf. Yellow bird's-foot trefoil and ladies bedstraw, pink spikes of common centaury, bright blue milkwort and tiny white flowers of fairy flax all grow together in a close-knit mat of vegetation; there may be as many as 30 different kinds of plants growing in a piece of turf no bigger than a coffee table. The flowers are so prolific that it is not easy to find a place to sit; just when you think you have succeeded, you may well discover that the spot you have chosen is already occupied by a stemless thistle – a plant that makes up in prickles what it lacks in stem.

All around are low hummocks capped with wild thyme and the exquisite flowers of eyebright; these hummocks are anthills, a common feature of this long-established grassland. I have often watched green woodpeckers feeding here, probing the anthills with their long tongues. Once there was a grass snake basking on top of an anthill amongst the eyebright; it seemed strange to find it in such dry surroundings, but given all the insects that inhabit downland turf it is probably a good hunting ground. Lizards can frequently be seen, and occasionally I have found slow-worms lying on the bare chalk rubble beside rabbit holes.

Dotted about the slope are tall spikes of viper's bugloss, a strikingly beautiful flower with its mixture of blue and pink. Where the turf is grazed right down by rabbits, yellow wort and centaury grow in profusion. Here, too, there are the bright yellow flowers of rockrose and the occasional adder's-tongue fern. Amongst the mat of carnation sedge and quaking grass is a mass of salad burnet; one of the loveliest chalkland plants with its delicately serrated leaves and tiny globular flowers, it has long been appreciated for its culinary qualities.

But it is the orchids that steal the show. In some years the slope is covered with them. Common spotted and fragrant orchids are most abundant, and there are plenty of twayblades too. Here and there are bee orchids, sometimes singly, often in small groups, each flower an exquisite imitation of a bumblebee. Then there are fly orchids, tiny plants that are easily overlooked, with several deep purple flowers which resemble minute velvet teddybears. In one spot is a patch of man orchids with yellowish flowers of distinctly human form. As the fragrant and spotted orchids finish flowering, their place is taken by deep-red pyramidal orchids, which have a curious fox-like odour. Later, in August, the same slope is covered in purple spikes of autumn gentian. The old flower heads will still be there next spring when the violets and cowslips emerge.

*The diminutive but exquisite fly orchid grows on several of the chalk downs around the southern fringe of London.* David Goode

Part of the attraction of downland, especially on warm, south-facing slopes, is the richness of insect life to be found there. Wherever you step the turf is full of grasshoppers, and you only have to sit for a few minutes to witness a wealth of different forms of the invertebrate world going about their business. The butterflies are particularly attractive and at certain times are very abundant. Some patches of chalk downland in London support a surprising number of different butterflies. In one small area 27 species have been recorded by the Kent Trust for Nature Conservation, including several that are becoming nationally rare.

Each of the remaining areas of downland in London has its own particular charms. Riddlesdown provides some fine views, and there is a sense of isolation on this wooded scarp. Open places on top of the hill retain patches of the old downland turf, full of rockrose and marjoram. If you are lucky, you might also find yellow rattle and an uncommon relative of the meadowsweet called dropwort, both of which are very rare in the London area. There are patches of kidney vetch too, which support a local population of small blue butterflies. This is also one of the few places in London where marbled white butterflies can be seen, a small colony having been established in recent years. The marbled white is a most handsome insect with its black and white markings and distinctive lazy flight; it is well worth seeing when on the wing in July.

Farthing Down offers a more open vista and conveys a stronger impression of traditional downland. It is in fact a landscape of great antiquity. Some of the hedgerows in this secluded corner of London date from Saxon times, and there are burial grounds of similar age. Traces of much older tumuli along the downland ridge suggest that the hill has been occupied by man for several thousand years.

The view from Farthing Down along Happy Valley is one of the finest country scenes in London. But the downland slopes are suffering the same fate as so many others: they are gradually being invaded by hawthorn bushes. It is a fine sight when all the hawthorn is in blossom and yellowhammers sing across the valley; but if the hawthorn goes unchecked for long the open downland will be gone for good, and with it all the chalkland flowers — so the City Corporation, which manages the area, is systematically cutting back the scrub.

At the end of March 1985 there was a party of wheatears here. They were obviously on their way north and did not stay long, but I was delighted to see these smart birds in their spring plumage on what was once their natural breeding ground.

Happy Valley and Devil's Den are well worth a visit on a warm summer's day. The grasslands are full of unusual flowers, including round-headed rampion, dropwort, horseshoe vetch and sainfoin, a plant which was once popular as a fodder crop. A remarkable feature of some of the slopes here is the abundance of great hay rattle, a rare relative of the yellow rattle, which is found in few places in Britain. At least a dozen different kinds of orchids grow here too, including the strange bird's-nest orchid, which can sometimes be found under beech trees in Devil's Den Wood.

# ◆ HEATHS AND COMMONS ◆

HEATHLAND AND COMMON was once a familiar feature of the countryside around London, particularly in places with rather poor soils where there were deposits of sand and gravel. Much of the original oak woodland in these areas was cleared long ago, and for centuries the heaths served an important function as rough pasture for cattle, sheep and horses. The sandy soil was covered in heather, gorse, bracken and rather poor grassland.

Although commonly regarded as wastelands by many including William Cobbett, who described Hounslow Heath as 'bad in soil and villanous in look', the heaths in fact supported a rich variety of wildlife whose needs were compatible with the traditional uses for grazing and cutting of whin. A century ago most of the commons which are

Opposite *Heathland vegetation has long since disappeared from Blackheath in Greenwich. The ponds were once used by cattle as they were driven to market in London.*

now within the confines of London were wild open spaces where nightjars and butcher birds were familiar, and stonechats, yellowhammers, whitethroats and linnets were found in abundance. Even the Dartford warbler was breeding on Wandsworth Common and on heathland in Kew Gardens until about 1880, and odd pairs were still seen on Wimbledon Common in the 1930s. This species was first identified as a British breeding bird in 1773, when it was discovered at Bexley Heath near Dartford. Sadly it has been ousted from many of its earlier haunts and only survives in any numbers on the heathlands of Dorset and the New Forest.

At the beginning of the nineteenth-century 16,650 acres of common land were recorded in Middlesex alone, much of which was open heathland. During the next 50 years, large expanses of common were converted to farmland, only to be overwhelmed by the tide of urban development which swept out from London across the surrounding countryside. But many of the surviving commons were protected and remain as open spaces within urban areas. Some are still genuine heathlands, supporting heather, gorse and birch trees, but the vast majority now have the appearance of town parks. At Clapham, Peckham Rye, Streatham and Tooting Bec the commons have become no more than expanses of grass with hardly a vestige of the original heathland vegetation. Most of the inner London commons, including Blackheath at Greenwich, have suffered the same fate.

Even Hampstead Heath, perhaps one of the best loved of London's open spaces, has lost its original heathland character. Walking over the heath today, it is difficult to believe that it was once covered by heather and gorse and supported bilberry and other heathland specialities such as petty-whin, dyer's greenwood, spotted orchid and clubmosses. We know exactly what the heath used to be like from a list of plants observed in 1629 by a group of botanists on the first recorded botanical ramble in the London area, details of which are included in Richard Fitter's book *London's Natural History* (1945). In the wetter places there were sphagnum bogs with the attractive pink-flowered bog heather and the white heads of cotton grass. Marsh pennywort, bogbean and even the insectivorous sundew grew in these bogs.

The Hampstead Heath of today is very different. The greatest change occurred in the early nineteenth century, when sand quarries were cut into large tracts of land; one of the original trackways across the heath, known as the Spaniards, now stands as a raised causeway high above the excavated areas on either side. Some of the quarries were 25 feet deep and so extensive that little of the original heathland vegetation survived. In another example of change, brick rubble can be seen along paths across the heath where debris from wartime bomb sites was used to fill sandpits dug to fill sandbags during the blitz.

Many of London's heaths have been excavated over the years to meet the insatiable demand for gravel. Excavation often started on a small scale, with the lords of the manors opening pits to provide gravel for road-making and building. But in postwar years the gravel industry has grown massively, with the result that whole areas of common have been totally destroyed. Hounslow Heath and Mitcham Common have suffered in this way, and there is continuing pressure elsewhere for what is referred to as 'gravel winning'.

In the interesting case of Mitcham, encroachment on the common was viewed with concern even a hundred years ago – yet huge changes went ahead notwithstanding and little of the original heathland now remains. The common's gradual demise is described in an article written in 1971 by the eminent Surrey botanist Ted Lousley. In 1765 Mitcham Common covered about 900 acres but was steadily reduced by enclosure to its present 440 acres. In the mid-nineteenth century it was dissected by two railway lines and, also at that time, its surface was covered in small gravel pits. When a further railway was proposed in 1877, public opposition was aroused, and both this and a proposal to expropriate 100 acres for a sewage farm were defeated. In 1883 an attempted encroachment at Beddington Corner led to the setting-up of an influential 'Committee for the Protection of Common Lands and Open Spaces in Mitcham, Beddington, Wallington and Neighbourhood'. This was followed in 1891 with an Act of Parliament giving powers to the Mitcham Common Conservators.

Although the committee was established to prevent unauthorised removal of gravel and to safeguard the common, it can hardly be described as a success. Owing to lack of funds, it was forced to accept activities which continued to damage the common. One of the first decisions of the conservators was to grant a licence for golf to be played on the common. The new golf club spent thousands of pounds in draining and filling marshy ground and bringing in soil to fill the gravel pits. In the process, much of the natural character of the heathland was destroyed. More recently, extensive areas of the open common have been used for the disposal of household refuse, and huge mounds have been created, no doubt to break the monotony of the featureless waste.

Only a century ago Mitcham Common was described as 'one of the most picturesque rugged pieces of country in the neighbourhood of London'. In 1911 Dr H. F. Parsons listed 460 species of plants growing there, a figure far higher than for either Hayes or Keston Commons. Now most of the common is rather nondescript grassland. Some of the heathland plants have survived in isolated pockets – ironically, many of them around the edges of the fairways on the golf course. But, although the common's original character has been almost totally destroyed, all is not yet lost. With sympathetic management, parts could be restored to heathland, especially at the northern end, where a number of heathland specialities still survive and a certain wildness prevails.

The natural features of London's heaths and commons have also suffered from the lack of grazing animals. Victorian paintings of Londoners taking the air on Hampstead Heath include scenes with cattle resting under the ancient oaks and flocks of sheep on Parliament Hill Fields. In fact there were sheep on the heath as recently as 1952. On Mitcham Common, too, there used to be substantial grazing. In 1874 one man was fined ten shillings for grazing too many sheep; he had apparently had 700 on the common for a period of six months. In 1909 the Conservators sought an injunction to restrain Henry Bankes, who claimed rights as a commoner, from turning out cattle, horses, sheep and other animals. Apart from the occasional grazing of horses, this practice has long since ceased.

As the heathlands of London were enclosed by new urban developments, so the traditional uses gradually died out. Grazing had kept all the trees and scrub woodland in check; when it ceased, some of the commons became birch or oak woods. Remnants of the original open heath can still be seen in the form of gorse and bracken, or even bushes of hawthorn, in clearings between the trees. Chislehurst Common, for example, is mostly birch and oak woodland with patches of heath around the edges. The same applies to others, such as Barnes and Keston Commons, though open spaces can still be found there. Even Wimbledon Common has been colonised by extensive areas of birch and oak, and the open heathland is now maintained by artificial means. But Wimbledon is by far the most rewarding of London's surviving heaths; it supports a remarkable variety of heathland fauna and flora.

*Many of London's commons are becoming colonised by scrub woodland. Here at Keston the open heath with ling is giving way to patches of rowan and birch.*

Wimbledon Common, together with Putney Heath, is one of the largest open spaces in Greater London, totalling some 1100 acres. That these commons have survived as wild heathland is largely due to the action of commoners in the 1860s when the then lord of the manor, Lord Spencer, proposed to 'improve' most of the area and turn it into a public park. Opposition to his plans led to a board of conservators being set up in 1871 to manage the commons of Putney and Wimbledon. Since then, although grazing has gradually declined and public recreation has taken its place, these commons have retained their natural character to a remarkable degree.

An early morning walk over Wimbledon Common after the willow warblers and tree pipits have arrived in April is one of my greatest pleasures. It has been estimated that over 100 pairs of willow warblers nest on the common; I can well believe it, for among the birch trees you are never out of earshot of their song. The tree pipits make themselves known more directly by their delightful parachute display, from the top of a tree down into the heather or bracken. Periodically there is the ringing call of a green woodpecker; recent records suggest that about 8 pairs of these handsome birds nest on the common. There are about 12 pairs of pied woodpeckers too, though being quieter birds they are rather less conspicuous. Redpolls are in evidence among the birch trees and, very likely, you will hear a cuckoo calling.

*Bell heather, dwarf gorse and heathland grasses at Keston Common.*

Walking northwards from the windmill, you cross open areas of bracken and heather with small clumps of birch trees scattered here and there. Wetter parts have patches of purple moor grass and mosses with heath rush and bog heather. These are the most extensive tracts of true heathland in London.

At this time of year few of the heathland plants are in flower but by June there are patches of yellow tormentil. Tiny flowers of milkwort and heath bedstraw also appear between the carpets of mosses and heather. Delicate feathery flowers of bog bean suddenly open in a patch of sphagnum moss on one of the London's few areas of real bog. Dwarf gorse and petty whin can be found in some of the drier parts of the heath, where patches of purple heather make a fine sight in August. In autumn there is a great variety of fungi in the birchwoods and out on the heath.

*Wimbledon Common. Extensive tracts of open heath with patches of bog make this the most valuable of London's heaths for wildlife. It is one of the finest open spaces in the capital.* David Goode

*Bog on Wimbledon Common has a carpet of sphagnum moss where bog-bean grows among willows and reeds.* David Goode

*A row of old oaks on Hampstead Heath marks an ancient hedgeline.*

Wimbledon Common might be the best example of true heathland in London, but it cannot rival Hampstead Heath for the latter's variety of views and beauty of landscape.

Little of the original heath vegetation now remains at Hampstead; I am told that there is one clump of heather in a secret spot. Much of what is now affectionately known as 'the heath' was farmland of the Fitzroy Farm estate before becoming part of the public open space. The landscape has a fine mixture of woods and fields with pockets of bog and marsh. Some of the woodlands such as those at Ken Wood are of ancient origin, and many of the old oaks on other parts of the heath mark parish boundaries. Near Hampstead Gate you can still see parish boundary stones beneath the trees. Vestiges of old hedgerows remain on Parliament Hill Fields, and there is an old hedge and ditch marking the parish boundary between Hampstead and St Pancras. Further north near Ken Wood farmhouse is a sunken lane and five-bar gate, relics of the time when cattle were driven to the fields. But the heath is a curious combination of old and new. Much of the present landscape is derived from sandpits and brick fields of the nineteenth century, and many of the more interesting pockets of marshy ground have resulted from man's activities.

The intricate history of the heath is well described by Alan Farmer in his account of the heath published in 1984. The leaflet and map by Ralph Wade, published by the GLC, are also invaluable. The Heath and Old Hampstead Society arrange regular walks throughout the year with specialists on various aspects of history and wildlife. Bird walks are led by Kate Springett, the official bird recorder for the heath. During 1985 she noted 83 different species, of which 43 were known to breed, including great crested grebes, tufted ducks, kestrels, stock doves, tawny owls, lesser whitethroats, blackcaps, chiffchaffs, reed warblers and probably all three species of woodpecker. Places on the heath which are particularly good for birds include the bird sanctuary by the Highgate boating pond and the area around Viaduct Pond. The southern part of Ken Wood is also a good spot to see woodland birds and is a favourite place for people who feed the birds; several species of tits and even nuthatches may come to your hand for food.

A recent flora of the heath lists 200 species of flowering plants; as it excludes many groups such as grasses, sedges, mosses and ferns, the total could easily be double that number. Some parts are particularly interesting, such as West Field Bog, where a carpet of bog mosses in a shallow valley provides a habitat for very specialised species of both plants and animals. In a recent study of the spiders, Edward Milner found 3 species new to the London area, and others of note included the bog wolf spider. Efforts have been made to improve the bog conditions by cutting back the encroaching scrub. The nearby West Field has also been managed as a hay meadow rather than close-mown grassland to encourage a variety of meadow flowers and butterflies.

Other commons have their own particular wildlife attractions. Barnes has a pleasing mixture of birch trees and rough grassland; Keston Common has some fine patches of bell heather, and it is possible that adders survive on nearby Hayes Common. Heather is still abundant on the Addington Hills near Croydon. Ponds on some of the commons are important for breeding colonies of toads and newts, especially the palmate newt, which is now quite scarce in the London area.

The wildlife of some inner London commons is becoming more readily appreciated, with the publication of a nature trail guide for Tooting Common by the Borough of Wandsworth and an attractive booklet describing Clapham Common Nature Walk by the London Wildlife Trust.

# ◆RIVER AND MARSH◆

FEW NATURAL HABITATS have suffered so much at the hand of man as marshland. Bogs, swamps, fens and marshes have traditionally been regarded as treacherous disease-ridden wastes good only for reclamation. Wherever possible, they have been drained and put to more productive use, often – as the wilderness has been tamed – with a great sense of civic pride and achievement. Drainage of the marshes has

*Marsh marigold, an attractive plant familiar to many country dwellers two generations ago is now rarely seen in the London area as the marshes have disappeared.* David Goode

often gone hand in hand with river-improvement schemes. Artificial embankments and straightening of river channels to prevent flooding have enabled the marshes to be reclaimed and even used as building land. In London, not only have the Thames-side marshes been largely reclaimed, but most patches along the numerous small tributaries have also disappeared. Virtually all of London's rivers are now confined within artificial channels and some, such as the Walbrook, Fleet and Effra, have been covered over completely, so that they now flow underground. But despite all the effects of increased drainage over the centuries, a few areas of marshland have survived and are among the gems of London's natural world.

In Roman times the banks of the Thames in London are thought to have been fringed by reedbeds with thickets of alder and willow. Even in what is now the heart of the City there were patches of marshland. A wide strip of marsh known as London Fen lay to the west of the broad tidal inlet of the River Fleet. Further downstream the estuary was bordered by extensive salt marshes. By the time William of Normandy came to Westminster the river had been embanked in places to prevent it from flooding. Crops were being grown quite close to the river in what is now Westminster and Stepney, though the Palace of Westminster itself stood on Thorney Island, one of the many small islands along the river, of which Bermondsey (Bermond's Isle) was another.

*The Silk Stream, a tributary of the Brent, near Edgware Road. Part of the original marshland became a tip, and recently a supermarket has been built on the land.*

Some patches of marsh survived for a long time, even in the immediate vicinity of the City. A plaque in Finsbury Circus, close to Liverpool Street station, records that this area 'was originally a fen on a moor known as Fensbury'. It was this area of ill-drained land just outside the City wall that gave its name to Moorfields. Culverts in the wall, built by the Romans to allow the Walbrook to flow through, gradually became blocked up, giving rise to an area of marshy fields. The fields were still there in medieval times and, when frozen over in the winter, provided a popular place for skating. Although partially drained during the reign of Henry VIII, the marsh remained until 1606, when its level was raised and it was laid out with walks, elm trees and benches, so becoming London's first public park.

A map of London in 1690 by Jacobus de la Feuille of Amsterdam shows the immediate environs of the city in some detail. At that time the built-up area north of the river extended from the present position of Wapping westwards to just south of Westminster, where a road led to the horse ferry which then operated across the river at Lambeth. To the north the city extended as far as Clerkenwell and Bunhill Fields, beyond which was open farmland. South of the river a large area between Lambeth Palace and Southwark was also open fields protected from the river by an embankment. On the south bank opposite Westminster there were no buildings, only woodyards along the river bank, and open fields beyond. Where Waterloo station is today was a patchwork of low-lying fields called Lambeth Marsh. The built-up area of Southwark just to the east was separated from this by a 'green wall' or earth embankment, from the presence of which it can be assumed that the marsh was still liable to flooding from time to time. Some of these marshy fields were still there a hundred years later. John Rocque's map of 1769 shows patches of marshy meadow by the lane called Lambeth Marsh and another wet area at the south end of St George's Fields where the Imperial War Museum now stands. William Curtis found flowering rush growing in St George's Fields some time towards the end of the eighteenth century but remarked a few years later that it had since disappeared as a result of improvements.

Late eighteenth-century maps of the London area show vast tracts of marshland along the Thames downstream of the capital. This was in fact grazing marsh, a kind of low-lying pasture used for sheep grazing, which had been created by reclaiming the intertidal salt marsh. Records show that Roger de Commerville started draining the marshes at Rainham in 1250. Since then the river has been progressively embanked along its entire length from London out to the estuary, enclosing the newly created pastures behind low sea walls. The fields were very wet in winter, and even in summer the land had to be drained by a multitude of ditches running between the fields. By Tudor times these grazing marshes supported enormous numbers of sheep and there was a major export trade in wool to Flanders and ewes' milk cheese to France. Wide expanses of these grazing marshes can still be seen out along the estuary in Kent and Essex; the landscape they create has a quality all its own.

Another map by Rocque (1762) shows areas of grazing marsh south of the river in Rotherhythe, opposite Wapping. The whole of the Isle of Dogs was grazing marsh too, from the village of Poplar southwards. Patches of salt marsh survived in places along Limehouse Reach and the river embankment here was referred to as the marsh wall. Marshland covered the peninsula east of Greenwich which now gives access to the Blackwall Tunnel. But it was east of here that the marshes started in earnest. A continuous tract of marshland stretched for 11 miles along the north bank of the Thames, from the River Lea at West Ham to the chalk promontory of Beacon Hill at Purfleet. In several places it was more than two miles from the river bank to solid ground across the marshes. In 1762 Abbey Marsh covered all the flat land south of Church Street, West Ham, right down to the Thames. Here there were numerous little fields separated by ditches, with winding marshland tracks following the old river walls. South of Plaistow High Street were the Plaistow Levells and further east the East Ham Levells. Beyond Barking Creek were Barking Level, Ripple Level, and Dagenham Marsh with its brackish lake known as the Dagenham Breach, which was formed when the area was inundated long ago by the sea. Some of the early maps show a duck decoy on the Dagenham Marshes. Eastwards again were the Hornchurch Marshes and beyond the Ingrebourne River the Rainham, Wennington and Aveley Marshes. South of the Thames was a huge area of marsh at Plumstead and Erith, most of which is now occupied by the new town of Thamesmead, and other areas of grazing marsh occurred alongside the mouth of the River Darent at Crayford.

Several names on some of the early maps provide a clue to previous conditions. An old sea wall is marked on early ordnance survey maps just south of the village of Plaistow, over a mile from the present edge of the river. Other names, such as Rippleside (now along the A13 near Dagenham) and Marshfoot near Rainham, indicate the previous extent of the marshes. The name Wallend is still used today just west of Barking. This was the end of the sea wall along Barking Creek and formed the landward edge of the East Ham level.

Rocque makes it clear that many of London's smaller rivers had extensive areas of marshland associated with them. The whole of the Lea Valley from Walthamstow down to the Thames was a continuous tract of marshland, including Walthamstow Mead, Leyton Marsh, Hackney Marsh, Bow Marsh and Stratford Marsh. Over in the west of London there were marshy fields and watermeadows along the River Crane in Twickenham. Marshy patches also occurred along the River Wandle in places such as Baggery Mead, which is now within the densely built-up suburbs of Merton.

In the early years of the nineteenth century the Isle of Dogs must have exhibited even greater contrasts than it does today. The West India Docks were opened in 1802, yet the southern half of the peninsula remained as farmland and sustained flocks of sheep until at least 1838. It was a genuine greenfield site when the Millwall Docks and Cubitt Town were built. The great new docks which made London so significant as a port were virtually all constructed on grazing marshes. Rotherhithe Marshes were the first to go, with construction of the Surrey and Commercial Docks, though there were marshy patches surviving in 1844, when the first ordnance survey map was published. By then, large parts of Abbey Marsh had been built over and the Victoria and Albert Docks had been constructed alongside the river on the Plaistow and East Ham levels. Even so, large stretches of marsh remained between the docks and the growing suburbs of Newham. Beyond Barking Creek the marshes were at that time still unaffected by London's industrial tentacles.

---

Opposite *Wilderness Island on the River Wandle at Carshalton. Ponds on the island were once used as fishponds and have recently been re-excavated to create a wetland nature reserve.* David Goode

South of the Thames, parts of the Plumstead and Erith Marshes were, by that time already being used by the Woolwich Arsenal, though the main development here was not until the turn of the century. An elaborate series of canals and moated islands was constructed, where explosives were developed and tested. Despite this, large parts were relatively undisturbed and a record of the wildlife is available from the writings of Richard Ruegg, who was a munitions inspector at the Arsenal during the 1840s. He knew the marshes well as a wildfowler and wrote a book called *Summer Evening Rambles Round Woolwich*, in which he described the pools and morasses which were the abode of mallard, teal, heron, snipe and lapwing. The surface was intersected with broad dykes and reedbeds where bitterns and bearded tits nested, and in winter the marshy fields were visited by vast flocks of snipe which 'thronged every pool and swamp in the field with such numbers that the effect of a discharge amongst them must have been prodigious'.

*Teasels and reeds on the Thames bank at Tripcock Ness.*

In the early nineteenth century, marshland birds could be seen in places remarkably close to the centre of London. In *London's Natural History*, Fitter refers to men who went snipe shooting in the 'Five Fields' just south of Hyde Park, before these marshy fields were drained in the 1820s and replaced by the mansions of Belgravia. More surprising, perhaps, was the presence of all three species of harrier in the immediate vicinity of London. In 1812 a pair of marsh harriers nested by an osier pond near the Surrey Canal between Bermondsey and Deptford, and a pair of Montague's harriers were shot in Battersea Fields. Nowadays both of these are extremely rare as breeding birds in Britain. The hen harrier, which still visits the Thames-side marshes in winter, was apparently known to hunt over the meadows along the Old Kent Road. At that time, too, bearded tits and spotted crakes were to be found in the reed and osier beds along the Surrey Canal, and reed warblers nested in reedbeds along the riverside at Battersea.

By the year 1900, bitterns and bearded tits had disappeared from the Plumstead Marshes, except as occasional visitors, and by then the great expanse of marshland along the north bank of the river was becoming affected by piecemeal development. During the course of this century, industry gradually extended further downriver. By 1931 most of East Ham level had been converted to a major industrial complex and other new industries were springing up along the road to the massive power station out on Barking level. New railway lines crossed the marshes too, serving the power stations and other new industries. The Ford Motor Works was built on Dagenham Marsh, covering virtually the whole of it, and the army took over parts of Rainham and Aveley Marshes for rifle ranges.

Since the Second World War industrial expansion, and dereliction, has continued apace. Of all the marshland that once existed along the Thames estuary, the only patches which survive today within Greater London are fragments at Rainham and Wennington, and their counterpart across the river at Crayford, (where the marshes have, so far, escaped industrialisation). Upstream of central London is another fragment of riverside marsh at Syon Park opposite Kew Gardens. Other stretches of wild and wet can be found along some of the tributaries of the Thames, but they are few and far between. One of the biggest of these lies along the valley of the Ingrebourne near the old Hornchurch aerodrome between Rainham and Upminster, where marshy fields and reedbeds are still regularly flooded in the winter. Patches of marsh also survive in the Colne Valley on the other side of London, but perhaps the most surprising is Walthamstow Marsh at the south end of the Lea Valley close to Hackney.

Rainham and Wennington Marshes extend for nearly three miles from Rainham railway station to the Mar Dyke at Purfleet. This is no longer a continuous expanse of marshland but a hotchpotch of habitats, including fragments of grazing marsh mixed in with rubbish dumps, army ranges and silt lagoons. Despite this, the area is host to a wealth of wildlife. Rainham and Wennington must now be one of the best places to see wetland birds in the immediate vicinity of London. The mixture of artificial habitats, together with the adjacent salt marsh and intertidal mudflats, provides an unusual variety of conditions. The grazing marshes and ranges offer a suitable breeding habitat for about 12 pairs of lapwing and slightly fewer redshank. About 20 pairs of yellow wagtails nest here, some of them in the pasture, others among beds of sea aster in dried-out silt lagoons. Reed warblers and reed buntings are abundant, nesting along the marshland dykes, and a few pairs of corn buntings nest on the army ranges. In recent years stonechats have suddenly increased from a single pair in the early 1970s to about 12 pairs. It must be a particularly good habitat for kestrels too, for up to 5 pairs are known to nest. Other nesting birds include several pairs of shelduck, which nest down rabbit burrows or in holes within the old buildings on the ranges. Recently, oystercatchers and little ringed plovers have nested on some of the older silt lagoons.

Considerable numbers of waders and waterfowl use the lagoons, especially during the winter, but also during migration periods. Of the waterfowl, teal are particularly numerous, with up to 4000 some winters. Up to 300 pintail duck and 500 shelduck have also been recorded. Throughout the winter from November to March waders which feed on the intertidal mudflats along the river use the lagoons as a roosting area. Up to 3000 dunlin may be seen flying in dense flocks from the river as the tide drives them off their feeding grounds. Large numbers of snipe feed within the lagoons throughout the winter, and for a couple of months before Christmas there is generally a resident flock of ruff, one of the more unusual waders to be seen here. This wader gets its name from the ornate plumage which it assumes in springtime when its ruffs and plumes are used in colourful courtship rituals – though it is far less showy in winter.

During the winter several thousand black-headed gulls scavenge for food on the refuse tip, and up to 10,000 use the lagoons and ranges for roosting. Herring gulls, blackbacks and common gulls occur in lesser numbers. The rubbish tip is also a great attraction to crows, especially in hard weather, when there may be up to 300 vying with the gulls for scraps of food. The marshes are still a winter haunt of the hen harrier and the day-flying short-eared owl, both of which hunt for voles.

During migration periods the silt lagoons attract a variety of waders, especially from July to September, when they provide a valuable stopping-off point for birds moving south. Little ringed plovers begin to arrive in July and seem to congregate here before proceeding on their southward journey. This is one of the less common waders breeding in Britain and the flocks of 50 to 100 birds are some of the largest known. Maybe the area acts as a gathering ground for birds nesting on gravel pits north of London. Other waders come from further afield. The diminutive bird known as the little stint is a regular visitor in the autumn on its way south from Siberia to Africa. A few turn up most years, usually with flocks of dunlin. In September 1978 unusually large numbers of these Russian migrants suddenly arrived, with up to 50 recorded on several days. Other waders which regularly appear at this time of year include substantial numbers of green and common sandpipers and small numbers of spotted redshanks, greenshanks, black-tailed godwits and curlew sandpipers.

The long-established grazing marshes of Rainham and Wennington also contain a great variety of aquatic vegetation including some notable rarities such as the golden dock, seaside crowfoot and a most unusual grass called procumbent poa which, once more widespread along estuaries elsewhere, is now largely restricted to a few localities around the Thames estuary and Hampshire coast. Such rarities do not occur simply by chance. They are indicators of the very special conditions that persist here.

Early in April 1985 I visited Rainham Marshes on a beautiful spring morning. As a colleague, Jacklyn Chandler, and I drove around the edge of the marshes along Ferry Lane, past outliers of Thames-side industry, the low sun cast long shadows across the wet fields. I was surprised to see a film crew already in action out in the middle of the marshes and, puzzled about what they might film in so exposed a location, we stopped to have a closer look. The huddle of film-makers formed a circle around a short-eared owl sitting upright on a post. It made a fine picture against the backdrop of factories. A wild owl in London's backyard – but, as we watched, it flapped a few times and we realised that it was in fact a tame owl which was firmly tethered to the post!

It was the only owl we saw that day on the marshes but there were plenty of other attractions. Red flags were flying over the military ranges so it was not possible to visit the lagoons and low-lying pastures on the landward side. Instead, we followed a safe route along the foreshore. Several pairs of lapwings were displaying over the sheep pasture and there were reed buntings singing from bushes along the dykes. Skylarks seemed to be everywhere and now and again there was the sound of a meadow pipit's song. A sudden commotion among the lapwing drew my attention to a large hawk-like bird which was hunting along the edge of a thicket of elder bushes. It was a female hen harrier, a winter visitor to the marshes which would shortly be returning to its summer quarters, probably on some Scottish moorland. It was a fine sight, beating low along the bushes then suddenly dropping to the ground to seize some unwary vole or other small animal. A kestrel appeared, hovering over the sea wall, and a swallow passed low over the marsh, the first of the year. It had a purposeful look about its flight, as if it still had a long way to go.

Approaching the elder clump, we came upon a grass snake basking in the sun among tussocks of long grass and last year's teasel heads. This was a warm spot sheltered from the east wind and already there were plenty of insects about. Small tortoiseshell and peacock butterflies were flitting between the bright-yellow coltsfoot flowers which covered the old rubbish tip. The coltsfoot must be a valuable source of nectar at this time of year and, as well as the butterflies, several large bumblebees were making the most of it.

*Grass-snake on the marshes at Rainham.* David Goode

Redshanks were calling with the lovely rippling song which you hear only on their breeding grounds. Every now and then several pairs of redshank joined together in a noisy party to circle the marshes, perhaps in preparation for establishing their breeding territories. A lone ringed plover called repeatedly from a patch of shingle over by the river bank, where perhaps it would nest, and nearby a group of shelduck made a fine spectacle with their smart black and white plumage. Later that morning four ladies appeared on the sea wall equipped with boots and binoculars. They were from an Essex field club and were regular visitors to the marshes. Their trip was made worthwhile by lovely views of the harrier. As we walked back to the car, a hen pheasant exploded noisily from the long grass and a pair of common partridge also took to flight, warning off everything around with their staccato alarm.

Back by the factories there was no sign of the film crew. They and their owl had departed, leaving the marshes to the redshank, lapwings and a lone harrier.

Crayford Marshes lie on the very fringe of Greater London between the last of the outlying housing estates and the meandering course of the River Darent. Travelling to the marshes from Bexley one comes upon them with remarkable abruptness. An invisible line, which is the edge of London's green belt, divides the marshes from the suburbs. From an unattractive postwar housing estate one passes into a country lane fringed with cow parsley, which drops down to run between water-filled dykes and buttercup meadows. Here is a low-lying landscape of marshy fields separated by wide ditches, for all the world like Romney Marsh or parts of the Somerset levels. Despite the skyline of smokestacks and industrial dereliction, the open vista creates a curious sense of isolation and freedom. Industrial effluents carried on the wind are a grim reminder of the upstream industrial belt, but the marshes nonetheless provide a great release from the claustrophobia of city life.

In May the fields are alive with the song of skylarks and meadow pipits as well as the incessant chatter of reed warblers along the edges of the dykes. As at Rainham some of the ill-drained fields provide ideal nesting habitats for yellow wagtails, lapwings and redshanks. During April and May you can hear the spring flight-song of the redshank and will very likely see one of these red-legged waders bobbing nervously from the top of a fence post as it guards its nest. Wherever you go in the marshes at this time of year the redshanks can be heard calling, making a sound that might be associated more with uplands of the north than with the East End of London.

The marshes are attractive to other birds too. Kingfishers and herons regularly fish along the dykes and in August green sandpipers drop in to feed as they move south. Throughout the summer the air is filled with flocks of swifts and house martins feeding on the multitude of midges. There is also a local population of swallows which nest in wartime pillboxes still dotted round the fields. In winter these same fields are a popular hunting ground for short-eared owls, and at that season flocks of linnets and gold-finches abound on the seed heads of thistles and other wetland plants.

---

*Opposite Marshland dykes and rushy fields where lapwing and redshank nest. This is the flat lying landscape of Crayford Marshes.*

Close to the sea wall the water in the dykes is distinctly brackish, but the other side of the marshes is a freshwater area. This contrast produces a surprising mixture and variety of species. The dykes just behind the sea wall are covered in seaside crowfoot, a rather unusual type of water crowfoot which grows only in brackish conditions and is now very scarce in the London area.

Along many of the dykes there are fringes of reeds and sedges with an abundance of fen and marshland plants. Yellow iris and pink valerian grow along the edges with bright blue water forget-me-not, and some of the dykes are covered in water crowfoot. In early summer the fields are yellow with buttercups – a sight all too rare these days. Towards the landward edge of the marshes old hawthorn hedges bordering the dykes have become overgrown and now provide sheltered enclaves rich in insects. Orange tip, wall and comma butterflies occur here, and southern hawker dragonflies can be seen hunting. At this 'freshwater' end of the marshes smooth newts can be found beneath the crowfoot and in places the banks are riddled with holes of water voles.

Walthamstow Marsh is the sole remnant of the vast tract of fen and marsh which once occupied the whole of the lower part of the Lea Valley. Most of this area, known as Hackney Marshes, has been drained and turned into innumerable football pitches. Fortunately, one small section of the marsh at Walthamstow was spared that fate, though even this 88 acres is chopped into three parts by railway lines. Within these areas there is a remarkable variety of fen and marshland habitats where over 300 species of plants and hundreds of different sorts of insects have been found.

At one time these marshes were lammas land. For most of the year (from Lammas Day on 13 August to Lady Day on 6 April) they were used by the commoners of Walthamstow as grazing land for cattle and horses. In the summer owners of particular plots had rights to take crops of hay. Some of the metal posts marking such plots can still be found. Nowadays parts of the marsh are cut for hay, leaving wetter areas to form beds of sedge, fen and reed. Patches of willow scrub have developed where silt was dumped on the marsh during construction of the Springfield marina fifteen years ago, but most of the marsh is much too wet for trees to become established.

Along by the river is a wide belt of comfrey and thick beds of reedmace and reed grass eight to ten feet high. In the south are extensive sedge beds, where 8 different kinds of sedge occur. Large areas are covered in meadowsweet and other parts in michaelmas daisies. Rough grassland is full of fenland flowers such as wild angelica, purple loosestrife, codlins and cream, ragged robin and yellow flag. Wetter places have great water dock and flowering rush. It is well worth a visit in July when the combination of colours in the marsh is at its most attractive.

Nearly 30 different species of bird have been recorded breeding in the marsh. Cock reed buntings are very much in evidence, easily recognisable from their black head and white collar, and there is an incessant chattering and chirring of sedge and reed warblers in the depths of the fen. Hundreds of swifts and martins feed over the marsh at times and, throughout the summer, there is the welcome song of skylarks.

July is a good time for marshland insects too. Even a short walk through the fen is likely to reveal a multitude of species, including colourful burnet moths and dragonflies and a variety of butterflies, grasshoppers and crickets. This is one place in London where you could well hear the strident song of the rare Roesel's bushcricket.

*Lots Ait at Brentford, one of several artificial islands on the Thames which have wildlife specialities such as the two-lipped door snail.* David Hope

Walthamstow Marsh has been referred to by some as the fen in the city. It is an apt description for it must now be the nearest genuinely wild place to the centre of London.

Along the upper reaches of the Thames, at Syon Park, there is a fascinating tract of marsh in one of the few places where the river is not embanked. The area is rich in marshland plants, among them wild angelica, purple loosestrife, meadowsweet, hemlock water dropwort and the introduced balsam commonly known as policeman's helmet. These marshes are also notable for their rare insects and snails. Clumps of willow scrub near the river are used as a regular roosting place by large numbers of herons. The area is private, but can be seen from the Thames bank at Kew.

It is easy for small patches of long-established marsh to be overlooked. The significance of one such area by Duke's Meadow has only recently been fully appreciated. This patch, known as Duke's Hollow, lies by the Barnes railway bridge, at another point where the river is not embanked. The marsh includes such botanical specialities as hemp agrimony and marsh ragwort, and supports the rare turreted snail known as the 'two-lipped door snail'.

Further upstream by Richmond there is a belt of fen and marshland plants on the river bank by the towpath. Purple heads of loosestrife make an attractive picture here, along with codlins and cream, marsh ragwort, reed grass and hemlock water dropwort, all of which are growing out of the stone pitching which forms the river bank. From here to Teddington weir the river is overhung by trees with hardly a house in view except for the modern flats and boatyards of Eel Pie Island. It is a very different vista from that associated with the tideway in central London.

From my office window opposite Westminster I have been aware of the daily flight of cormorants moving up and down the river. Occasionally they are to be seen fishing near Lambeth Bridge, which would have been unheard of several years ago. During March 1985 three shags appeared on the Thames in central London fishing between Hungerford and Waterloo Bridge and roosting on a stone abutment of Hungerford Bridge. When the lakes in the Royal Parks freeze, flocks of tufted ducks suddenly appear on the river just outside County Hall. Sometimes they will feed here for several days – a good indication that the river is much cleaner now than it once was. It is even becoming common for anglers to fish from the steps by County Hall, where they catch dace and chubb.

*Purple loosestrife, reed grass, hemlock water dropwort and marsh ragwort by the Thames towpath at Richmond.* David Goode

Thirty years ago the Thames was so polluted that the whole stretch from Richmond to Tilbury was normally completely devoid of fish, except for eels. During the 1950s few waterfowl were to be seen on the river within London, but the clean-up operation during the 1960s had a dramatic effect. By the late sixties and early seventies huge rafts of wildfowl could be seen in winter on the Thames between Woolwich and Rainham. In 1972 there were 4000 pochard on the river at Woolwich, with sizeable flocks of tufted ducks, mallard and teal. Pintail, too, were fairly numerous, and it was common to see several hundred shelduck.

*Flocks of tufted ducks feeding on the Thames at Westminster during severe weather when park lakes are frozen.*

These huge concentrations of waterfowl may have depended partly on the substantial supply of invertebrate food in the mud, especially tubifex worms. As other invertebrates gradually became established, so the numbers of wildfowl declined, but it is still possible in winter to see flocks of pintail, wigeon and teal on the river between Tripcock Ness and Rainham. The mudflats at Barking Creek are a favourite place for waterfowl, including waders such as redshank, lapwing and dunlin, and nowadays cormorants fish the whole stretch of river from here to Wapping.

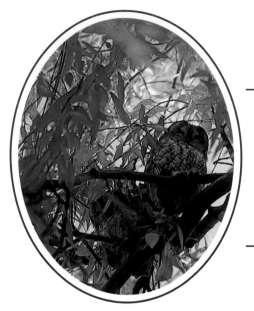

### ✦TWO✦

# THE
# MAN-MADE
# WILD

# ◆RAILWAYS◆

THERE is something about travelling by train in London which brings a totally different perspective to the city. For a start, many of the railway lines form leafy corridors which seem remote from the surrounding urban sprawl. Here there is a sense of isolation and freedom from the hubbub of congested city streets. But it is not just more relaxing to travel this way; there is also so much more to see. Travelling by train is an excellent way to appreciate London's natural life. In many places the railway cuttings and track-side land have become so overgrown as to take on a feeling of countryside which sometimes persists well into the centre of town. The line from Croydon to London Bridge is a fine example of this. For miles it runs through a continuous swathe of greenery until it suddenly emerges at New Cross Gate into a broad vista of central London, passing between the rooftops and chimney pots of Bermondsey, with the towering office blocks of the City just beyond.

Even where railways run along seemingly endless backs of dreary houses, with inevitable piles of rubbish tipped over walls, nature manages to thrive. Herbaceous borders of goldenrod and fireweed clothe the embankments, while wallflowers and buddleia cling to crevices in the brickwork. Wherever they have the slightest opportunity, wild flowers colonise the railwayside, producing an ever-changing panoply of colour. The banks also provide a refuge for other wildlife. For a regular traveller, the unexpected glimpse of a fox, or of a kestrel quartering the embankment in search of voles, brings a little magic to the day. The most direct contact that many city dwellers have with the seasons may be what they see from a train window on the way to and from work.

After the drab browns of winter the first real sign of spring may be a sudden profusion of bright-yellow coltsfoot, which seems so much at home on the clinker and coal dust of old railway sidings. Late March is also the time for pussy-willow. Bushes of willow and sallow seem to grow readily on disused railway land and their soft yellows bring a welcome touch of colour to the bare landscape. Patches of primroses spring up here and there, and hard on their heels come the cowslips. Both these species have been picked out of existence from many of the woods and meadows in the

London area, but some have survived, especially on inaccessible railway banks. One patch of primroses and cowslips on a steep cutting through the chalk south of Purley has spread noticeably in recent years. Now, hundreds of tiny cowslip spikes can be seen towards the end of April. Another spring flower which favours the wooded railway cuttings is the celandine, which seems to survive even amidst tangled growths of ivy and produces yet another splash of yellow at this time.

There are changing colours on the railway banks throughout the year: primrose and celandine provide a splash of colour in springtime, while everlasting pea (right) flowers in August. David Goode and Tony Hare

By May, bluebells can be seen among the ubiquitous railside sycamores; pink and white flowers mingling with the blue betray their garden origins – no doubt they have spread from bulbs cast over the wall with the garden rubbish. Bluebells are not alone in this; in fact, a large number of plants which have successfully colonised railway banks originated in gardens. Honesty is one of the more spectacular; in early May some stretches of the railways are positively purple with this native of the Near East.

As buds break and leaves appear on the trees, railway journeys in London take on a new dimension. All is suddenly refreshingly green and lush. Birch scrub which stood stark throughout the winter is clothed in soft green foliage. Even where railways run high above the terraced streets of inner London the scene is transformed as plane trees spring into leaf amid the chimneypots.

Towards the end of May, some of the railways are white with hawthorn blossom, particularly in the outer suburbs, where postwar building on farmland left hedgerows along the railway intact. Nowadays the hedges have become overgrown bushes and trees, which make a fine sight at this time of year. An old adage suggests that 'Kissing is in season when the gorse is in flower' – for, of course, you can nearly always find the odd flower braving the cold even in midwinter. But the gorse is at its best in early June, when it produces a blaze of yellow where the railways pass through heathland soils. Cuttings north of Chislehurst on the Orpington line are covered in gorse, and it can also be seen along the railways at Mitcham Common and Hounslow Heath. There are even patches mixed with bracken growing on the railway banks near Wandsworth Common, though the gorse here must be only a vestige of its former glory, as the common lost its genuine heathland character long ago.

Every year early in June there used to be a marvellous display of lupins by the big railway junction north of Croydon. They covered a huge area of disused sidings, where the mixture of pinks and blues was quite magnificent. It seemed likely that they had spread from the gardens of two railway cottages which had once stood in the middle of the junction. Sadly the construction of a new railway flyover has recently destroyed most of the lupins and now the vista is mostly grass and concrete. But a few patches have survived and maybe they will spread again to cover the new embankments.

While the may is in blossom the railwaysides are also white with cow parsley, its tall umbrella heads forming a continuous border to the track. Two weeks later, these flowers are gone and the ox-eye daisy seems to be everywhere. But among all these white flowers there are occasional splashes of colour. One may catch a glimpse of the pale pink of wild roses, or the brilliant yellow cushions of stonecrop, and by now other plants, such as the tall dock-like leaves of horseradish and blue spikey flowers of comfrey, are beginning to appear.

July and August are the most colourful months along the railways, the time when beds of deep-red rosebay willowherb cover the banks. Nowadays, fireweed is such a familiar plant, especially on wasteland, that it is difficult to believe it was scarce a hundred years ago. No doubt its proliferation along the railways has been assisted by its windborne seeds being carried in the wake of passing trains – and, with the prevalence of burned patches along the banks, the fireweed seems to have found its ideal habitat.

Another striking sight at this season is the sprawling garlands of large bindweed and everlasting pea which festoon railway banks and brickwork. Brockley station boasts one of the best shows, the deep-red flowers of the pea and large white trumpets of bindweed combining to produce a magnificent wild garden. Elsewhere are tall purple thistles and, by now, cow parsley has been replaced by its taller relative, the hogweed. On grassy banks bird's-foot trefoil and yarrow can be seen, and patches of marjoram cling to the steep cuttings through the chalk. Where lupins grew a month earlier, there are tall spikes of evening primrose, a native of North America now well established in the wild. Its pale yellow flowers open only in the evening, when it is visited by moths seeking nectar, but nevertheless it makes an attractive picture with its tall spikes along the disused sidings.

In high summer, tree-lined sections of the railways have a lush feel as sunlight dapples the dark green foliage. The deeper cuttings are covered in ferns and there are places such as the stretch of line between Teddington and Fulwell where bracken dominates. But still more flowers appear. In August the deep-purple fronds of buddleia adorn countless nooks and crannies of the ageing railway buildings. Famous as the butterfly bush, buddleia certainly provides an important food source for insects, and even in central London you can find peacock, small totoiseshell and red admiral butterflies feeding on its flowers. On occasion, while waiting for trains at Clapham Junction, I have seen all three. Buddleia is another plant of foreign origins; it was introduced from China less than a hundred years ago, but has taken well to our urban wastelands.

While buddleia adorns the brickwork, the railway banks become covered in golden-rod, an incomer from North America. Like honesty it has spread from gardens, and along the embankments its golden-yellow fronds are often mixed with the red of rosebay willowherb. By now, there are seedheads on the thistles, and one can often catch glimpses of parties of goldfinches perching on the thistleheads. Red berries on the rowan trees are another reminder that autumn is approaching.

By September and October it seems that only one flower prevails – the michaelmas daisy, which brings a soft blue haze to the railside. Another garden escape, this particular introduction from North America has been with us for nearly 300 years. Virtually all the flowers that are particularly abundant along the railways are from foreign parts; for relatively few of our native wild flowers thrive in this artificial environment.

*Michaelmas daisies on the Devonshire Road nature reserve in September.*

By this time of the year it is the trees which provide colour. The soft yellow of the birches by the District Line tube near Gunnersbury is stunning in the autumn sunlight. Gradually the colours die, but even in winter, after the snow has gone, there is beauty in the shrivelled leaves still hanging on the gaunt branches of oak trees – or in the shining bark of silver birches and in the soft brown stems of last year's reeds still standing on the banks, their feathery tops silhouetted against the sky near Brockley station.

Observing the countryside along the railways is an education in natural history. Quite apart from the passage of the seasons, there is always the unexpected: a jay flying into the trees near Forest Hill in Lewisham, magpies building their nest in a trackside hawthorn bush near Finsbury Park, a heron standing motionless by the River Brent in Ealing – even a pied woodpecker on its undulating flight among the birch trees at Streatham Vale.

The line from Wimbledon to Carshalton provides several glimpses of the River Wandle near Morden Hall, and then again at Wilderness Island by Hackbridge. Here are fine views across the strange open landscape of Beddington, where lapwings tumble in aerial displays and ponies roam at will in the rushy fields. As the train stops at Mitcham Junction, only twenty minutes from Waterloo, there are times when the air is full of the song of skylarks. In May, the blackcaps sing in the leafy cuttings of the line through Crystal Palace, and the wooded slopes near Chislehurst are full of bluebells. On the other side of London the line to High Wycombe runs beside another bluebell wood at Perivale; beyond are the fields and hedgerows of Horsenden Hill, patches of countryside in the suburbs of Ealing. Further out on the same line are fine winter views of wildfowl on the flooded gravel pits by the River Colne.

I think that the most dramatic winter sights are to be seen from the North London or Hertford line near Walthamstow. Here the railway runs on a causeway between reservoirs and, especially in frosty sunshine, there are magnificent views of the winter flocks of ducks, gulls, cormorants and grebes. In spring, too, there is plenty to watch, with the coming and going of countless herons in one of Britain's largest heronries (see page 75). Nearby, the Cambridge line snakes its way round Walthamstow Marshes rich with the pinks and blues of codlins and cream, and comfrey.

Further east, on the fringe of London, between the Dagenham car factory and the petrol tanks of Purfleet, the line to Tilbury crosses a wild landscape of dykes and marshy fields. This area is one of the last vestiges of the Thames marshes. Here in winter you may glimpse a short-eared owl hunting by day, or flocks of waders ousted at high tide from their muddy feeding grounds on the river standing motionless in the fields. Here too is one of the earliest places to see flocks of winter thrushes on their arrival from the far north, and redwings and fieldfares feeding on berries along the overgrown hedges. In springtime you might even see redshanks displaying over the fields or standing guard on a fence post in the marshes. They take little notice of the trains, and it is often possible to see these shy birds at surprisingly close range, even if it is only momentarily.

Some of the stations can also be exciting. I have frequently seen kestrels hunting over Clapham Junction, and on winter evenings there is a regular flight over the station of herons in ones and twos heading westwards towards Barnes. Clapham Junction is a favourite haunt of the black redstart, a small robin-like bird which chooses to nest in rather dilapidated buildings. While waiting for a train at Clapham I have often listened for its characteristic song and have occasionally been lucky. But with the constant noise and rush of trains there are not many silences long enough to pick up its intermittent call. In fact, there is a danger of missing your connection if you become too engrossed.

The eastbound platform at Berrylands, a suburb of Kingston, commands a fine view of the adjacent waterworks, and commuters waiting for their morning train may well see flights of duck or waders such as snipe dropping in to feed on the sludge lagoons of the sewage works. In winter a profusion of gulls and waterfowl can be seen from the station. Other stations have quite different charms. At Highgate you may hear green woodpeckers calling from the nearby woods or blackcaps and willow warblers singing from birch trees along the disused railway by the station carpark.

◆

*Buddleia and brambles have colonised this disused railway maintenance yard at Drayton Park station.* David Goode

Some stations have their own special treasures. The suburban line from Moorgate in the City travels underground at first, emerging into the open at Drayton Park station, which boasts an unusual array of wildlife. Here beside the station, flanked by high walls, is a somewhat derelict area that was once used as a railway maintenance yard. Now its deep concrete-lined inspection troughs are full of bracken and the yard is covered in brambles and buddleia bushes. Despite its location, the place is full of wild flowers and butterflies.

When I visited the yard at the end of July 1985, an abundance of red clover and the tiny yellow flowers of hop trefoil were providing a great attraction to butterflies. There was a profusion of meadow browns and small skippers, as well as several bright-red burnet moths, which seemed out of place in such an urban scene. Fronds of buddleia were covered in small tortoiseshells, and red-tailed bumblebees visited the tall yellow flower spikes of mullein. In one corner I found a patch of feverfew, an attractive flower of the chrysanthemum family which has long been used as a medicinal herb to 'drive off the fever'. Originally a native of Turkey, it has now become a common plant of waste places. All over the decaying concrete surfaces were leaves of coltsfoot, suggesting an attractive picture in early spring, when this plant's yellow rays must

*The old Broad Street station demolished in 1985 was a remarkable haven for wildlife with black redstarts breeding and a family of foxes living under one of the platforms.*

brighten an otherwise desolate scene. In view of the dereliction, I was not surprised to hear that this is another place favoured by the black redstart. Apparently the bird has nested here regularly for the past ten years, save an unaccountable absence in 1984. It seems that British Rail unintentionally offers a wide choice of nesting places for this bird, which is still a considerable rarity as a breeding species outside the London area. Drayton Park caters for other birds too. When I was there, the air was full of house martins and swifts feeding on airborne insects that had recently emerged from this miniature nature reserve, while parties of goldfinches explored thistleheads within a stone's throw of the station platform.

The old Broad Street station must have qualified as one of the strangest wildlife spectacles in the whole of London. Sadly, it has gone now to make way for a massive new development next to Liverpool Street, but in spring and summer 1985 it was an extraordinary sight. A large part of the station had been disused for many years and here, under the shadow of the NatWest Tower, in the heart of the City, was a veritable sanctuary.

I first visited the station early on Good Friday morning, in the opening week of April, and as I passed through the ticket barrier I heard the soft song of a willow warbler coming from a thicket of buddleia between the platforms. This tiny migrant had just arrived from West Africa on its way to some northern birch wood. It was strange to hear such a sound in central London.

As the bird flitted away over the railway tracks, a hush fell on the station. Apart from the occasional train on the North London line, it seemed deserted. Then several cock blackbirds began to sing, staking out their territories. As I walked down the platform, I was surprised to disturb a small flock of linnets and goldfinches among the buddleia bushes. A pair of dunnocks were courting on top of the ornamental brick-work of the old station wall and, as I watched, another small bird flitted up to the top of the roof. The sooty black body with white patches on the wings was unmistakable: it was a cock black redstart, another recent arrival from the south, but this one seemed here to stay. It sang a few times from its vantage point on the wrought-iron, occasionally quivering its red tail, then flitted off across the station to the signal-box roof. Again I heard its characteristic rattling song. It looked very much at home and would no doubt find a place to nest in one of the many holes in the brickwork. This bird seems to like old walls; on the continent, old town walls provide one of its favourite nesting sites.

*Catkins of aspen at Broad Street station, April 1985.*

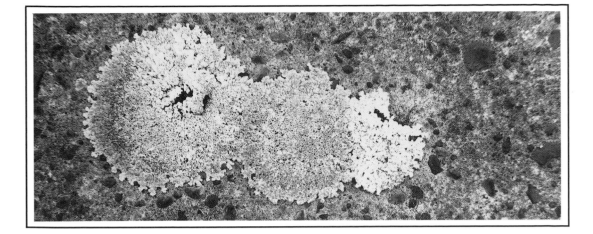

*Lichens on the concrete platform at Broad Street station.*

Between the platforms flowering willow trees made a splash of soft yellow, and even at this early date bees were visiting the flowers, including several large bumblebees. An aspen tree growing on the railway track was also in flower, its beautiful long grey-green catkins pendulous among the tangle of buddleia. In places the concrete platform was encrusted with lichens, and clumps of bracken were putting up new shoots between the railway sleepers.

As I went back into the station, I caught the familiar whiff of a fox and, sure enough, there were tell-tale droppings on the platform. Not far from the ticket barrier was a large hole under one of the platforms and from the smell it was obvious that foxes were in residence. Another visit about a month later confirmed my suspicions, and one evening in May I was lucky enough to see cubs playing on the disused railway tracks. Alan Mackenzie, the signalman, had been aware of the foxes for some time. He often noticed them in the evenings, but one day a linesman working on the track in the middle of the day saw a fox run past him only to disappear under the platform.

My last visit to the station was late in the evening on 26 June. Despite the roar of a mechanical digger demolishing the walls, a black redstart was still singing from the rooftop and I only hope it raised its brood in time. I think the foxes had already departed.

Railways are, of course, one of the best places to find foxes in London, and it is quite likely that you will spot them in broad daylight. The first railway foxes I remember seeing were just south of East Croydon station. I was travelling south on a crowded commuter train one evening in May. As we stopped at signals in a cutting, a deep City voice suddenly boomed through the soporific compartment, 'The hunt's not doing its job very well.' Just outside the window, on the embankment, a vixen was feeding small cubs in the soft dusky sunlight. It was a magnificent sight, and she seemed totally unconcerned by our proximity. I shall never forget her sharp eyes gazing down at us and the cubs jostling under her for milk.

Since then I have always kept a watch for foxes at various places along the railways where I know they are likely to be. In 1984 one family of cubs was raised on a bank near Streatham Vale station, and others between Brockley and Forest Hill. Quite often in May I would catch a glimpse of cubs tumbling on the embankment or of the adults lying out in the sun. Frequently someone on the train was provoked to comment in surprise at seeing wild foxes so far into London. But in some places commuters have become quite used to such sights, especially during hard winter frosts. During January 1985, when there was a deep covering of snow, foxes living near Grove Park station were frequently spotted crossing the tracks beside the platform. One regular traveller told me he had never seen a fox so close except in a zoo.

Some patches of railway land have been protected as nature reserves, even alongside working railways, and here it is possible to see in more detail the plants and animals of the railway banks. At the Devonshire Road nature reserve in Lewisham (see page 178) there is an attractive mixture of habitats on the gently sloping embankment between Forest Hill and Honor Oak Park. Chiffchaffs sing from the taller trees and there are patches of scrub with open grassy glades. Bullfinches, goldfinches, long-tailed tits and jays are all common, and kestrels can frequently be seen hunting over the reserve; they are thought to nest in a nearby church steeple. Common lizards and slow worms bask among the anthills on a sunny slope; they may also be found under bits of rubbish such as car wheels or old tiles. Slow-worms favour the open conditions of the railway embankments; I have noticed them on the disused railway line in Sydenham Hill wood, on railway banks in Finchley and along the chalky cuttings near Coulsdon.

In north London the old railway which used to connect Finsbury Park station with Alexandra Palace has been turned into a footpath called the Parkland Walk which wends its way through the suburbs of Hornsey and Highgate. A rich variety of wildlife occurs on the old railway banks and cuttings. Spotted flycatchers nest in places in the brickwork of the old bridges, and 17 species of butterflies have been recorded, including the silver-washed fritillary, holly blue and orange tip. It is a most attractive walk. Further north the disused railway from Mill Hill to Edgware now provides another 'railway walk'. Here there are wooded cuttings with oak and hawthorn and a host of wild flowers, including enchanter's nightshade, wood avens, great burnet, toadflax and burnet saxifrage. Part of this old railway track is now managed as a nature reserve by Dollis School.

# ◆ WATERWORKS AND RESERVOIRS ◆

UNTIL THE LATE nineteenth century there were very few large ponds or lakes in the London area. The Serpentine in Hyde Park and the lake at Osterley were two of the largest ornamental lakes. There were the Pen Ponds in Richmond Park, and Highgate Ponds by Hampstead Heath, but none of these was very large. The only sizeable water bodies were three reservoirs at Elstree, Ruislip and Brent, which served as feeders for the Grand Union Canal. The last of these, often known as the 'Welsh Harp', was built in 1835 and was by far the largest, extending to nearly 200 acres along the valleys of the River Brent and its headwaters. A few other water-supply reservoirs existed near Walthamstow and Stoke Newington, and beside the Thames at Lonsdale Road in Barnes.

Since then, however, numerous large reservoirs have been constructed to cater for the capital's insatiable water demand. Now there is a string of reservoirs along six miles of the Lea Valley between Walthamstow and Enfield Lock, and a whole district of lakes in the Thames Valley near Heathrow airport, several of which are over a mile across. In total, they amount to some 3500 acres of water. A series of new aquatic habitats has thus been created, which, together with the flooded gravel pits of the Colne Valley, has had a profound effect on birdlife in and around the capital.

Around the turn of the century several of these large reservoirs were completed, including those at Barn Elms, Walthamstow and the first two big reservoirs at Staines.

---

*Dense flocks of coot congregate on many of London's reservoirs in winter.* Anthony and Elizabeth Bomford

It seems that some birds quickly took advantage of these new habitats. According to Macpherson, who recorded the effects of these new reservoirs on London's birdlife in 1927, blackheaded gulls adopted Barn Elms as a roosting area as soon as the reservoirs were completed in 1897. These gulls had only become abundant as winter visitors to London in the previous few years, when they apparently used the Londsale Road reservoir and Chiswick Eyot on the Thames to roost. After a visit to Barn Elms in February 1902, Cornish provided a vivid description of the tightly packed mass of gulls covering an acre of ice. In the remaining areas of water there were about 70 tufted duck and coot and, to his surprise, 2 great crested grebes. These were the early days of colonisation. Four years later 80 of the birds were seen at one time on the larger reservoirs at Staines. At Walthamstow Reservoir the first pair of great crested grebes nested in 1904 and, in the following year, a pair of tufted duck; by 1914 herons were nesting on an island in the middle of the reservoir.

As the years passed, substantial winter populations of waterfowl became firmly established. In 1937 an organised count of waterbirds in the London area revealed a total of 6569 birds of 13 species excluding mallard duck. These included nearly 2500 tufted duck and about 1500 coot, 853 teal, 744 pochard, 272 wigeon and 234 goosanders. By then, the total number of grebes had risen to 385. One of the specialities of London's waterfowl at that time was the smew, a delightful duck of the sawbill family which breeds in northern Russia. The drake smew is a most elegant bird, delicately marked in black and white. A few first appeared on Barn Elms Reservoir in 1922, and during the count of 1937 a total of 51 were recorded. In particularly severe winters larger flocks were sometimes seen; during the exceptionally hard weather of 1947 a flock of 78 was at Barn Elms and another 125 at Molesey. Hard weather affected other wildfowl too. Richard Fitter remembers 'a vast pack of nearly two thousand pochard and tufted duck huddled together on Barn Elms in the cold spell of 1938–39'.

London's birdwatchers soon realised that there was more to the reservoirs than the wealth of winter wildfowl. Despite the urban surroundings, these reservoirs also provided a stopping-off point for a surprising variety of avian visitors, especially during the main migration periods in spring and autumn. Barn Elms became a Mecca for weekend birdwatchers, who were frequently rewarded with the sight of some unusual vagrant. Great northern divers and Slavonian grebes, a velvet scoter and Temminck's stint, spotted redshanks and black-tailed godwits, even grey phalaropes and pratincole – all of these and many more were seen during the 1930s and 1940s at Barn Elms, in the midst of a heavily built up area, only seven miles from St Paul's.

The story is much the same today, except that there are rather more birds and a lot more birdwatchers. So popular has birdwatching become that the Thames Water Authority has produced a pamphlet, *Birdwatching at Reservoirs*, giving details of those reservoirs available for birdwatching and how to obtain a permit. A charge is made for an annual birdwatching permit, in much the same way as for angling or other forms of outdoor recreation, but so far it is rather less than for comparable permits. The leaflet lists 62 birds which can regularly be seen at the London reservoirs, and the birdlife of each reservoir is briefly described.

Thirty years ago birdwatching was regarded as a somewhat eccentric pursuit. Nowadays it is commonplace to see people carrying binoculars while out for a walk. At the reservoirs, some go simply to savour the spectacle of hundreds of waterfowl in the winter sunshine. Others are more interested in spotting rarities than in enjoying the view. Alternatively, there are some dedicated ornithologists who regularly watch particular places. Every week they systematically count the flocks of several thousand gulls and waterfowl on the reservoirs. The data collected by such people forms part of a national scheme run by the Wildfowl Trust to keep track of numbers throughout Britain. The counts, which began in the 1930s and have continued every year since (except during the war), provide a vast amount of knowledge about the number of wildfowl wintering in London.

In 1974, R. C. Homes, who first organised the counting scheme in the London area, summarised the changes that had occurred over the previous 25 years. He found that there were regularly over 10,000 birds during the winter on reservoirs, gravel pits and lakes, and nearly double that number in periods of hard weather. Some species had definitely increased over the 25 years, while one or two had declined. The average number of tufted duck, the commonest diving duck, had increased from about 2000 in 1950 to nearly 5000 by 1972. Dabbling ducks showed a good deal of variation in numbers but the shoveler had definitely increased from about 100 to nearly 400 birds. Since the early seventies the numbers of shoveler and goldeneye have continued to increase, and gadwall too have grown in numbers to the point where they are now commonly seen on many of the reservoirs.

Not long after the Nature Conservancy came into being in 1949, the reservoirs at Barn Elms were designated as a Site of Special Scientific Interest on account of the waterfowl populations. These reservoirs still form a valuable wildlife sanctuary in this part of London. In recent years there have been flocks of nearly 200 shoveler and over 100 teal together with large flocks of diving ducks. During July and August several hundred tufted ducks use these water bodies as a safe refuge while moulting, and during hard winter weather it is possible to see large flocks of pochard and tufted ducks. Barn Elms is also popular with a variety of other waterbirds, including cormorants, which have become a regular feature. It is strange to see in the suburbs of Barnes a group of these ungainly birds flying low over the rooftops. On occasions quite large numbers of them congregate to fish at the reservoirs, as in December 1983, when 65 were seen at one time. Another common bird here is the coot, which gathers in flocks of several hundred. But the most abundant bird at Barn Elms is still the black-headed gull, which uses the reservoirs as a nightly roost (see page 149).

If I was asked to pick my top ten natural wonders of London, the heronry at Walthamstow would certainly be one. With well over 100 pairs this is now the fifth largest heronry in Britain. It must also rank as one of the strangest, being entirely surrounded by the built-up areas of Tottenham and Walthamstow. The herons nest in trees on two small wooded islands in the reservoirs just south of Ferry Lane. In this part of the Lea Valley, herons can often be seen passing overhead, but during the nesting season there is a constant procession of birds on their way to and from their feeding grounds. To see the heronry itself, you have to obtain a permit from the water authority, and it is well worth the effort: a visit while the birds are on their nests is an unforgettable experience.

Herons are early nesters. They start to stake out their territories in the dead of winter. Each male bird calls from his selected nesting site to attract a mate, a single strident far-carrying cry repeated at intervals. Once they have paired, it takes the birds about a week to build their bulky nest of sticks and twigs. Very often they will use a nest from the previous year, just adding some reinforcement and a new lining. Some lay eggs even in February, and most of the colony is well advanced by March. But it takes nearly a month for the eggs to hatch, and I remember one evening visit in mid-April when many of the birds still seemed to be sitting on eggs.

*It is not unusual to see herons fishing in Central London parks. A few nest in Regent's Park and the heronry at Walthamstow is one of the largest in Britain.* Eric and David Hosking

That April evening I sat on the reservoir bank about 100 yards from one of the herons' islands. With the evening sun behind me it was a fine vantage point from which to see their comings and goings, as well as all the rituals which are part of their colonial way of life. One of the first things that struck me was the noise. A continuous succession of calls filled the air, but these were quite unlike the familiar melancholy bark of a heron in flight. This was a medley of calls, some guttural, some subdued and strangely musical, others high-pitched yelping notes that carried far across the water. In the background was a continuous clattering of many bills and an occasional louder 'clack' as one of the birds saw off an intruder. I had not realised before that the language of herons involved such a varied vocabulary. The colony produced a mixture of sounds which was reminiscent of an old-fashioned farmyard.

As individuals arrived back at their nests, there was a noisy greeting ceremony between each pair similar to the 'scissoring' of bills between pairs of gannets when they greet each other on the nest. It has been suggested that birds which nest in close proximity to one another need such rituals to identify their own mate from all the others in the colony. The herons seemed to have all kinds of rituals, some to do with courtship and others concerned with defending their particular patch. Each of these involved a different call.

From where I sat I could see 36 nests and there were obviously many more. Some were built in the very tops of the trees, others in the lower branches and even in the bushy underscrub. It seemed as if every possible nesting place was occupied. In among the branches the heron looked an ungainly bird. What a contrast to the stealthy hunter in the marsh that moves so slowly through the water – then, quick as a flash, spears a fish with one blow. Here in the treetops, the herons seemed out of their normal element, moving from branch to branch with difficulty. A bird returning to one of the higher nests tried to perch on the topmost twigs of the tree. Swaying precariously, it held out its wings to steady itself. Gradually it made its way in a series of inelegant jumps onto the nest.

I noticed that, as each bird came in to land, it would first glide slowly round the treetops with its neck fully extended, gradually lowering its legs and adopting an almost upright posture in preparation for landing. I could even see the small patches of feathers on the leading edge of the wings raised as flaps to stop the great birds from stalling as they came in to land.

Standing on their nests the herons looked very smart indeed with their distinctive black head plumes and beautiful slate-grey wings. Some nests were occupied by single birds quietly incubating eggs, but others were full of activity. Several pairs indulged in mutual preening or courtship displays with much bill clattering. One off-duty bird spent a long time tugging at a nearby branch, perhaps in the hope of adding it to the nest. Every now and then a pair of herons suddenly took to the air in a strange wild flight around the treetops before settling down once again on their nest. The heronry reminded me of a spectacular colony of egrets and night herons that I saw years ago in a remote part of Turkey; this one in London was all the more impressive because of its unlikely situation.

*Canada geese are now regularly to be seen in parks and reservoirs around London.*

As I walked back to Ferry Lane that evening, parties of cormorants flew over on their way to roost on other reservoirs further up the valley. A few were already perching in trees on one of the islands where up to 100 may congregate at times. A pair of Canada geese were nesting at the foot of a pollarded willow, and the drake made sure no one approached too near. Tree sparrows, which are not particularly common in the London area, were nesting in some of these old willow trees. The first sand martins and yellow wagtails of the year had arrived and several common terns were hawking around the reservoir.

Like Barn Elms, these reservoirs are designated as a Site of Special Scientific Interest, largely on account of the heronry. But they are also important for a variety of wintering and breeding birds. About 10 pairs of great crested grebes nest and, in recent years, both tufted ducks and pochard have been particularly successful. Two years ago tufted ducks raised 26 broods and there were 12 broods of pochard. As with Barn Elms, these waters provide a place for tufted ducks to congregate while moulting. Apparently there were 1300 of them in the Lea Valley during August 1983. In winter there are sizeable flocks of diving ducks, dabbling ducks and coots.

Throughout the year there is always something of interest to see at Walthamstow Reservoirs. People in north-east London are lucky to have them on the doorstep. But for many birdwatchers the larger reservoirs at Staines near Heathrow aiport are more popular. Here it is possible to view the large concentrations of waterfowl from a public causeway between the two reservoirs where there is no need for a permit. In recent years the water level of one of the reservoirs has been lowered, exposing acres of mud, which is much favoured by waders and dabbling duck, especially teal. At other times the reservoirs are a stronghold for diving ducks. A few years ago counts during November revealed 5000 pochard and 4000 tufted ducks, some of the largest concentrations of these species in Britain.

A Sunday morning in winter is quite an experience out on the causeway. The medley of calls from distant waders and waterfowl is punctuated every few minutes by the roar of an aircraft taking off from Heathrow. Flocks of lapwing and teal take flight occasionally, but on the whole the birds seem unconcerned. Along the causeway there may be 100 birdwatchers with telescopes trained on the birds. This is a good place to see birds in migration too. In both spring and autumn a variety of gulls, terns and waders make their appearance, and I shall never forget the spectacular arrival, one evening in the first week of May, of several thousand swifts just back from their winter sojourn south of the equator.

The Welsh Harp or Brent Reservoir near Hendon is very different. It lies in the shallow valley of the River Brent, which was dammed 150 years ago to provide a feeder reservoir for the Grand Union Canal. Over the years it has gradually silted up and is now a shallow lake with a remarkably natural appearance. The northern arm, fed by the Silk Stream, has extensive areas of reedbed and thickets of willow, and there are similar areas of marsh where the Dollis Brook flows in.

From a carpark by the bridge over the reservoir in Cool Oak Lane a path runs southwards along the edge of the water. Fine old willows grow along the bank and in summer yellow flag provides a splash of colour in the shallows. The people who live in the row of semi-detached houses backing onto the reservoir here have a delightful view

The Welsh Harp or Brent Reservoir, an important wetland habitat in the suburbs of west London. Parts are now managed as a nature reserve where up to 30 pairs of great crested grebes nest. Dollis Brook (right), which flows into the reservoir, has provided a nesting site for king-fishers.

across the reed-fringed water, with the distinctive shape of Wembley stadium on the skyline beyond the dam, and the spire of St Andrews at Kingsbury rising above the willows on the far bank. The path leads to a wide shallow bay fringed with reedbeds and dotted with clumps of willows. Although most of the reservoir is used regularly for sailing, especially at weekends, this marshy bay and much of the shallow northern arm of the lake provide sanctuaries for waterfowl. So important are they for wetland wildlife that these parts of the reservoir are now treated as nature reserves.

When I visited the lake recently in spring, large numbers of grebes were congregated in the marshy bay. To see more than one or two pairs of great crested grebes on a stretch of water is quite unusual, yet here there were 30 pairs or more. This colonial nesting of grebes has become one of the specialities of the Welsh Harp, and is certainly one of the more unusual wildlife sights of London. Apparently the birds form what is now one of the largest single colonies of grebes in the country. This is all the more surprising when one considers that not so long ago grebes were extremely rare. In early Victorian times the plumage of great crested grebes was much in demand for the millinery trade. Feathers of the ornate crest and ruff were particularly sought-after, and grebes were hunted almost to extinction in Britain to meet the demands of fashion. It is thought that in 1860 there were only 42 pairs nesting in the whole country, and at that time none was to be seen in the London area. Since then, partly as a result of bird protection laws in the late nineteenth century, the population has gradually recovered. By the turn of the century, grebes were nesting in Richmond Park and Osterley, and 30 years later they could be found in over 20 places around London. Since then their recovery has been helped enormously by the large number of newly created lakes resulting from sand and gravel workings. Now there are at least 200 pairs breeding within twenty miles of St Pauls, and they are even nesting successfully in several of the central parks. The recovery of the grebe has certainly been one of the most spectacular increases in wildlife to be witnessed by Londoners this century.

Walking round the reservoir that spring morning, I was joined by Leo Batten of the Welsh Harp Conservation Group, who has done a great deal to improve conditions for wildlife at the reservoir. He explained how parts of the marsh, which were becoming covered in willow scrub or thick beds of reedmace, had been carefully excavated to create shallow lagoons, so providing new feeding areas for the waterfowl. New islands had been created and reedbeds planted to provide a mixture of habitats. A score or more nesting rafts had also been installed in the middle of the bay, to encourage terns and other birds to nest. As we walked by, a heron stood preening on one of these platforms and other rafts were occupied by a variety of waterfowl. They are obviously well used and seem to have been remarkably successful as artificial nest sites. Several pairs of common tern have already used them, and they are also popular with the commoner waterbirds such as mallard, coot, moorhen, tufted duck and Canada geese. Many of these species also breed elsewhere in the marsh along with pochard, dabchick, shoveler and possibly even gadwall. Canada geese are showing signs of a rapid increase as a result of improvements which were originally intended for other waterfowl.

Efforts are also under way to encourage herons to nest. Platforms have been erected in some of the willow trees to provide sites, suitably equipped with plywood models of herons to act as a lure. Apparently this was done successfully in the Camargue nature reserve in France to establish a new colony of egrets. Perhaps a tape recording of calls from a heronry would also help!

As we squelched through the marsh, the scent of watermint filled the air. A reed bunting called and several snipe flew off on our approach. In winter this is a favourite place for jack snipe, a smaller and much rarer relative of our common snipe best known by its habit of dropping down into cover again almost as soon as it has flown. In summer here the reedbeds resound to the song of sedge and reed warblers, and in other marshy places around the banks of the reservoir the delightful flowering rush can still be found. A little further on we passed a small pond, one of many which the conservation group have dug in the marsh to provide suitable conditions for frogs, toads and newts, which were not so long ago much reduced in numbers. Apparently the digging of ponds and reintroduction of spawn has been a great success and now there are thriving populations, especially of newts. These ponds also provide valuable new habitats for dragonflies and other aquatic insects which are sensitive to the effects of pollution in the reservoir itself. All this conservation activity is gradually reversing detrimental changes to the wildlife of this area which have occurred progressively over many years. Who knows, perhaps even grass snakes, which local people remember seeing 20 years ago, will one day return to these marshes.

The spot where the Dollis Brook joins the reservoir does not look much like kingfisher country, but, despite the lack of suitable banks for nesting holes, a pair tried to nest here in recent years. They burrowed under a log in a shallow bank, but unfortunately their nesting place was too often disturbed by people for them to be successful. There are hopes that, in future, kingfishers will use artificial banks specially provided out in the marsh. Where the footbridge crosses the brook, other problems facing waterbirds on an urban river are all too apparent. Here there is a special trap to collect the floating debris and oil carried down the river. At times there is a terrible stench of oil and all manner of trash floats in the thick oily scum covering the surface. Most of the oil is diverted into a sump by the side of the stream to be removed at regular intervals by the water authority. Seeing the concentration of effluent that comes down the stream makes one wonder how kingfishers survive at all. Before this trap was built, all the pollution went straight into the reservoir, and there is no doubt that its erection has had a tremendous effect in improving the environment.

As we left the marsh, chiffchaffs and willow warblers sang from trees along the Dollis Brook and a pied woodpecker flew across to one of the willow clumps. Jays called and there was the sound of dabchicks trilling on one of the lagoons. Here on the edge of the reservoir, in the shadow of a tall office block occupied by a micro-electronics company, we were only a stone's throw from the big junction on the North Circular Road at the beginning of the M1 motorway.

Even quite small reservoirs and waterworks in heavily built-up parts of London support a variety of waterfowl. The Hogsmill works near Kingston is one example of this, and even the concrete tanks of the waterworks tucked in among the terraced streets of Surbiton are used by a surprising number of ducks and gulls, including black-backs and herring gulls. One of the oldest of London's reservoirs, at Lonsdale Road by the Thames in Barnes, is now managed as a nature reserve and there have been suggestions that two small reservoirs of similar age along Lordship Road in Stoke Newington should also be transformed into nature reserves or wildfowl parks now that they are no longer required for water supply. There is no doubt that the considerable wildlife already found on these reservoirs could be greatly enhanced by imaginative management to produce a most attractive wild spectacle in this densely built-up area.

In August 1982, one of the GLC's landscape architects suggested to me that a derelict waterworks in Hackney might be of some interest for wildlife – and, since there was some possibility that the Lea Valley Park Authority might buy the area from Thames Water, it would be worth having a look to see what was there.

The place in question was a set of old filter beds on a narrow neck of land between the River Lea and the new Hackney Cut, downstream of Lea Bridge Road. Built in 1852, these filter beds were used to purify water from the nearby reservoirs before it passed into the drinking water supply. In operation for over 100 years, they eventually closed in about 1969, to be replaced by modern filter beds at the Coppermill Road waterworks.

Because of its position in the Lea Valley, it seemed likely that the area would be a good place for birds. I know that many working filter beds attract gulls and waterfowl in winter, but I was not prepared for the changes which could occur in such a place once it is totally abandoned.

As I approached the filter beds along the canal towpath, the prospect did not seem very promising. A derelict power station, partially demolished, loomed high on the far side of the canal, and beyond were tower blocks of flats. In the other direction several football matches were in progress on the vast expanse of grass that was once Hackney Marshes. True to the fashion of Victorian waterworks, the site was protected by a remarkably ornate and annoyingly high brick wall. But I could hear sounds of waterfowl, and a heron drifted overhead and dropped out of sight to land somewhere beyond the wall. There was no obvious way in. The only way I could satisfy my curiosity was by climbing on top of a high concrete block.

My eyes met a scene of total tranquillity. In the foreground were several large ponds fringed with reedbeds; beyond were thickets of willow. Mallard ducks, coot and moorhens were out on the water and the heron stood erect by the reedy margin. House martins flitted over the water catching insects, and a large brown dragonfly darted to and fro. Several reed warblers were singing from the safety of the reedbeds and a party of goldfinches were feeding on the rough grassland just below the wall. A kingfisher flashed across the water and vanished over the embankment by the River Lea. Overhead a kestrel hovered for a while, then settled on a nearby electricity pylon.

It all looked so natural that it was difficult to believe that this was a derelict waterworks. But the concrete edges of the tanks were visible enough and it was clear that the scene had been created by natural colonisation. It struck me that, had I wanted to create a wetland nature reserve here, I would have been hard put to do better.

On a later visit I discovered a hole in the fence used by birdwatchers and local people who enjoy the solitude of the place. Then it was possible to examine the vegetation in more detail. Strangely, each of the old filter beds was colonised in a different way. Some were mostly open water with just a fringe of reeds, while others were completely colonised by fen and marshland plants with little water remaining. One was entirely occupied by a thicket of willows and black poplar with a variety of fen plants underneath. Not only were these different conditions of interest in themselves, but many of the plants which had become established were unusual in the London area. I later learned from a report of the Hackney Group of the London Wildlife Trust that, after the filter beds fell into disuse, sand and gravel was removed from some of the tanks but not from others, thereby creating the variation in water depths. So, quite unintentionally, a wonderful range of habitats was created.

Five different sorts of willow trees occur in the patches of carr, including crack willow, grey willow and common osier. The self-seeded hybrids of black poplar are of particular interest, as there are few examples known in Britain. Notable among the fen plants are tussocks of false fox sedge and tall fronds of great water dock. In places there are patches of fool's watercress, and beds of water mint produce a wonderful aroma. In open areas you can find the dainty pink heads of cuckoo flower – maybe, in time, this will provide the orange-tip butterfly with a suitable new habitat, as cuckoo flower is one of its preferred food plants. Clumps of common spike rush and greater pond sedge have become established in some of the filter beds, and the beautiful tall flower spikes of purple loosestrife are abundant. The nettle-like leaves of gypsywort can be found almost everywhere. The lovely spreading flowers of water plantain grow along the water's edge. Another attractive flower that likes these muddy margins is the nodding bur marigold. Both kinds of reedmace occur in the reedswamp, along with common reed and canary grass. There are even beds of true bulrush. Among the reeds are patches of hemlock water dropwort, a rather poisonous plant of the umbellifer family, and in places the banks are pink with the flowers of codlins and cream, otherwise known as great hairy willowherb.

Over a period of little more than ten years, some 30 different marshland plants have colonised the filter beds, creating a colourful mixture of wetland habitats from scratch. I wonder how far the birds were responsible. No doubt they brought in a number of aquatic plant seeds which helped to speed the process.

During the winter of 1982–83 I visited the Hackney filter beds regularly and found a surprising variety of birds. One morning the whole place was full of snipe, which must have arrived overnight. As I walked round, so they left one by one. I counted twenty-eight before I left. Another time there was a flock of lapwings resting on the open ground beside the tanks. Regularly there were small flocks of mallard, teal, pochard and tufted duck on the water, which were sometimes joined by groups of shoveler and gadwall duck. Herons occasionally settled on the concrete edges of the ponds and kingfishers were frequent visitors.

But the most exciting birds to arrive in recent years were two pairs of little ringed plovers, which took up residence during June 1984. At that time the water level of the ponds had dropped, exposing areas of gravel and mud, an ideal habitat for this particular species. It was marvellous to be able to watch the courtship displays and songflight of these plovers in the urban environment of Hackney, four miles as the crow flies from St Paul's. One of the pairs produced a clutch of eggs but they were so often disturbed that they eventually deserted the nest. By that time, the filter beds were much more easily accessible because part of the wall along the towpath had collapsed. Since then, the area has become less of a sanctuary for birds, more of an unofficial wetland wilderness for many local people.

Plans are being devised to create a nature reserve on part of the old sewage works at Beddington a few miles west of Croydon. This is one of the strangest landscapes in the whole of London. A patchwork of old settling beds used for disposing of sewage sludge covers an area of flat lying land well over a mile across. After periods of rain many of the beds form shallow lagoons. Others, unused for many years, have become covered in rank growths of persicaria and beds of nettles ten feet high.

Beddington is a place of wide open vistas with factories and cooling towers on the distant skyline and, way off across the lagoons, you may glimpse the occasional train going by on the Carshalton line. Gaunt trees stand dead in shallow pools, great flocks of crows gather at times and everywhere there are horses. Groups of horses roam at will grazing the banks among the old lagoons. They are so wild as to create an unreal atmosphere; were it not for the great line of electricity pylons marching overhead, it could almost be the Camargue.

The old sewage farm is a popular place with birdwatchers. One I met on a Sunday morning was a local magistrate, another a film maker. Both enjoyed the sight of the first whinchats and yellow wagtails of the spring. That morning a pair of little ringed plovers were preparing to nest and several pairs of lapwings were engaged in their lovely tumbling flight above the spot where they would shortly nest in the lagoons. It was too early yet for swifts, but swallows and house martins were already hawking over the lagoons after insects. A high-pitched piping from one of the long-dead elm trees announced the presence of a lesser spotted woodpecker, a tiny sparrow-sized bird, which gradually made its way along the hedgerow trees into Beddington Park.

*Beddington sewage farm, a popular place for waders on migration in spring and summer. The numerous horses owned by gypsies are allowed to roam freely among the old sewage lagoons.* David Goode

In the next few years the vista will change dramatically, for gravel is to be extracted from beneath the old sewage farm. But long-term plans include the creation of an extensive marshland nature reserve.

# ◆DISUSED SAND AND GRAVEL PITS◆

ON THE SOUTHERN FRINGE of London, in the green belt, is a flooded sandpit which has been disused for many years. It lies beside the main London to Brighton railway, close to an industrial estate on the edge of suburbia. A huge sandwashing plant looms above in an adjacent quarry, backing onto which are the gardens of a line of semi-detached houses. A pipeline brings silt-laden water from the working quarry, and the flooded pit now serves as a huge settling tank for the sandwashings. The landscape is entirely man-made, yet the sandpit holds an abundance of wildlife and, whatever the season, there is always something worth seeing from the public footpath that overlooks it.

Over the years, trees and bushes have grown around the edges of the pit wherever they could gain a hold. Rushes and reedmace grow in the shallows, but along one side the edges fall sheer into deeper water. Where these sand cliffs are still exposed, they are riddled with the nest holes of sand martins, and in one place there is a larger hole where foxes regularly raise their cubs. The whole place is no more than a quarter of a mile across but it forms a remarkable wildlife sanctuary.

When I visited the railwayside sandpit at the end of March 1985, the water was almost devoid of birds. Only a week or two earlier, it had been covered by large flocks of gulls and ducks. Now only a few duck remained, together with the inevitable moorhens and coot. Winter was obviously coming to an end. In the nearby birch trees there was a continuous babble of birdsong, a low chattering reminiscent of a starling roost, but with unfamiliar musical phrases. As I approached, I heard a high-pitched flight-call and realised that a huge flock of redwings was roosting in the trees. The northern thrushes looked very smart in their spring plumage, with brilliant cream stripes over the eye and a splash of red on the flank. But what excited me most was their song, which I had never heard before. It resembled the chatter of linnets, punctuated by a fluty call. Here was a flock preparing for their northward journey to the willow-clad hillsides of Norway, or perhaps the lava fields of Iceland.

Meanwhile, in the willow bushes around the sandpit, a chiffchaff was singing. This was the first of the migrant warblers heading north: a clear sign that spring had come. A cock reed bunting called from the willows where it would shortly make a nest. Out on the water tufted duck and pochard looked settled to breed, and a pair of great crested grebes were engaged in their extraordinary courtship rites. With their crests fully extended, they faced each other and rose up to full stretch, as if walking on the water. One of them presented some rotting vegetation to the other – no doubt part of the ritual of nest building – and for a time they remained shaking their heads at each other. Around the sandy edges of the pit, bright yellow coltsfoot flowers were out in the early morning sun and celandines were flowering along the banks of a nearby stream. It was perhaps too soon to expect to see sand martins, but they would not be long in coming.

The martins generally return early in April. An advance party will sometimes appear briefly, apparently checking that all is well, and then disappear again for several days. Suddenly one evening they are all around the sandpit, in and out of the nest holes, claiming their territory. The air buzzes as they hawk low over the water catching insects. At about that time, too, the sedge warblers return, and from then on their incessant chatter can be heard from the sallows and reedy margins.

April is a busy month. Snipe regularly drop in to roost on the sandpit, and other waders too, on their trek back north. In 1983, to the delight of local birdwatchers, 7 avocets appeared one day in mid-April. Common sandpipers are more regular visitors, on their way to an upland stream in Scotland or the Yorkshire Dales, but they do not stay long. At this time of year you can sometimes catch the call of waders as they pass over London by night; to me, whimbrel and greenshank are birds of moorland mists and sphagnum bogs, which seem quite incongruous in suburbia, but it is lovely to hear them nonetheless.

Time appears to pass slowly at the sandpit during May and June. Broods of mallard ducklings suddenly appear; tiny yellow balls of fluff dashing about on the water. Later, there are young grebes, with their zebra-striped plumage, and the bizarre red-headed offspring of the coot. A pair of kingfishers have nested in recent years and their sharp call can frequently be heard as they commute between their nest hole in the sandy cliff and fishing grounds on a nearby stream. The banks of the stream are too shallow for kingfishers to dig a tunnel, and it seems that the sandpit provides the only suitable place in the vicinity. But they are better off than a pair along the canal in Hackney, which had to make do with a factory drainpipe for their nest hole.

In May the plant life of the pit starts to flourish. First the primitive fruiting heads of horsetails emerge, strange brown spikes springing up as if overnight, opening at the top into a delicate cone which bears a multitude of spores. They are closely followed by lush growths of cow parsley, and by now white dead nettle, stitchwort and red campion are flowering. All the hawthorn bushes around the top of the pit are suddenly covered in blossom. On warm evenings the pit is alive with sand martins flitting low over the water, and from time to time the air is filled with the screams of visiting parties of swifts. Swifts obviously regard the place as a good source of food, for they have travelled some distance from their breeding grounds. One such evening, when there were towering swarms of midges all along the footpath, I watched a dabchick nipping about on the water like a whirligig beetle, snatching insects off the surface. There was an abundance of food to be had, and the dabchick seemed resolved not to miss a single midge; this was easy pickings compared with its more usual practice of diving to feed among the submerged water plants. Mallard ducklings straight from the nest feed in much the same way, mopping up midges as fast as they can.

By late May starlings are already arriving in the evenings to roost in the willow thicket. Many are young birds, only recently fledged, and easily recognisable by their brown plumage. From now on the roost will gradually grow in size as more and more birds finish breeding. Later in the year the roost will be further supplemented by birds arriving from the continent.

In June the banks start to look more colourful with beds of blue comfrey and the delicate pink of wild roses climbing on the hawthorn. Down by the water's edge the yellow irises are in flower. Soon there will be pink flowers of codlins and cream, or great hairy willowherb growing just above the water line around the edge of the pit. On the higher banks, hogweed is in flower and there are bright yellow clusters of the large bird's-foot trefoil, which grows in wet grassy places and marshes. Other members of the pea family include common vetch with its pink flowers and the tiny blue flowers of the straggling vetch, known as hairy tare.

As summer progresses, there is a profusion of yarrow, ragwort, red clover and yellow melilot. Fireweed is starting to appear and velvet tops are forming on the reedmace. Every umbrella head of hogweed seems to be host to a cluster of bright-orange soldier beetles.

The most impressive spectacle of warm July evenings is the congregation of starlings. By now there are thousands of them covering the willow bushes in a dense black cloud and producing a continuous babble of noise. Flimsy saplings of willow and sallow sway and bend as countless birds try to gain a foothold. Even the outermost tips of the branches are covered and gradually they sag into the water, whereupon the unfortunate birds have to find a firmer place to roost. Every now and then the whole flock takes to the wing with a sudden roar. Among all this activity, a lone kingfisher crossing the water is reduced to insignificance.

But there are other birds to be seen. July is the time when some of the waders and other waterbirds start to move south; the autumn migration is under way. A few lapwings are generally the first to arrive early in the month and their numbers gradually swell until, by August, there may be two or three hundred; they are families of adults and young birds which congregate after breeding. These birds could well be from the surrounding countryside of Surrey and Kent, supplemented later perhaps by birds from further north.

About the middle of July a few black-headed and lesser black-backed gulls, which may have been away to continental breeding grounds, start to return. But, for me, it is the waders which are the more thrilling visitors. Maybe at first only the non-breeding birds are on the move, but soon there is a steady passage of sandpipers and other waders all heading south to their wintering grounds in West Africa. By far the most regular are green and common sandpipers, but greenshank are often seen too. Green sandpipers, with their distinctive fluty call, will have come south from Scandinavia, while the others may be from Scotland. Occasionally other waders appear, such as ruff and wood sandpipers – or even rarer visitors, in the form of spotted redshank and little stint, which may have nested north of the Arctic circle.

At this season you never know what might occur from one day to the next. In 1980 a spoonbill arrived on 12 August. It was certainly the glorious twelfth for the local birdwatcher who first spotted it. This elegant, white bird, with its long black spoonshaped beak, caused great excitement for the two days that it stayed. The nearest breeding colonies of spoonbills are in the Netherlands and it may be that this one had wandered from its normal migration route down the Atlantic seaboard. Or perhaps it had come from further afield. Young spoonbills are known to wander considerable distances. One once landed up in Scotland on its way south from Yugoslavia! Easterly winds often produce oddities at this time of year, and the sandpit is always worth an early morning visit after a strong easterly has been blowing.

Apart from the southward passage of birds, other signs of autumn are evident. By late August there are clumps of red berries on the rowan and haws are turning red on the thorn bushes. Hogweed, which dominated the scene a month ago, is in seed now and its leaves are withering fast. But its place is taken by another umbellifer, the wild parsnip; everywhere its pale yellow-green heads rise above the tangle of bramble and fireweed. In places along the footpath there are delicate mixtures of colour, similar to those in a cottage garden, with beds of red bartsia, yarrow, large hop trefoil and the golden yellow orbs of fleabane, all backed by the verdant growth of wild parsnips, up to six feet high. There is a mass of ragwort too, its golden heads covering the sandy banks, and occasional flowers of common vetch and creeping cinquefoil can still be found. Big brown dragonflies hawk to and fro along the edges of the lake, suddenly swooping with a whir of wings to hunt amid the multitude of midges along the footpath. Bright red darters also occur, often resting on the footpath or fence posts.

As September begins the sandpit is quite a spectacle, especially in the evenings. Most of the sand martins have raised their young and the air is full of their dashing flight, but a few are still feeding late broods in the burrows. They will be around for another week or two yet, in contrast to the swifts, which left for their winter quarters a month ago. But, as some birds depart, so others arrive. The starling roost has grown enormously. Dark clouds of starlings circle the pit in a display of aerial gymnastics, suddenly descending like a swarm of locusts to settle on the hawthorns, where they break into a waterfall of noise.

*Small tortoiseshell butterfly on ragwort.* Jacklyn Chandler

One evening a hobby appeared, a beautiful falcon like a miniature peregrine. It made a few wild dashes up and down the pit, scything the air with its long curved wings. Perhaps it would take an unsuspecting martin, but no – it was away as quickly as it came, beating southward.

That same evening 50 or more lapwings stood motionless around the edge of the sandbank with a small flock of black-headed gulls and a solitary black tern. The tern was another continental visitor resting in the sandpit for a while before continuing its journey. For some reason it was chivvied repeatedly by the lapwings, which seemed to have taken a dislike to this unfamiliar intruder. It tried desperately to settle at the water's edge with the other birds, but eventually was driven to roost by itself on the end of a floating pipeline.

As dusk fell, a fox appeared on the sandbank. A regular visitor at this time, it would spend a lot of time sniffing around on the sand, occasionally digging at the surface, apparently in search of food, though what it was after I never discovered. As it approached, the lapwings took off one by one. With soft cries they flew away into the gathering gloom to find a safer roosting place. Meanwhile, mallard duck and coot, which had been loafing on the sand, splashed noisily into the water and stood off at a safe distance from the fox.

A sedge warbler sang somewhere in the willow thicket and the babble of starlings continued unabated. Occasional martins still hawked over the water and the first bat appeared. Then from a distance came the sound of geese: an intermittent honking. Moments later a long straggling skein came in low across the sandpit. Just before landing they fell silent, and there was a final flickering along the skein as they positioned themselves to land. With a great swish 40-odd Canada geese hit the water and immediately burst into a great clamour. These were just a few of a larger population which use the pit regularly in the winter. As I watched, wave after wave of geese came in, always from the same direction, until the shining water was completely studded with dark forms.

Gradually the several hundred geese moved towards the sandbank and as a body walked resolutely towards the fox, which was still snuffling about some yards from the water, apparently totally uninterested in them. The geese stood silently in solid ranks facing the fox. What followed was one of the funniest wildlife spectacles I have ever witnessed. The fox took a few paces towards the herd of geese and, as one, they turned round. At least, their bodies turned; their heads remained resolutely facing Mr Fox, while their legs carried them back into the water.

As the light faded, herons dropped into the pit one by one, a harsh croak announcing each arrival. Alighting in the water, they stalked to the edge of the sandbank. There they remained, dotted around in the shallows, motionless and hunched, ready for the night. I counted 9 before I left. Above the pit the huge sandwashing plant was now illuminated by floodlights. The constant hum and rattle of machinery would continue into the night, but it did not seem to bother the geese and herons in their sanctuary.

By the end of September the number of teal and mallard duck is increasing. The teal are noisy and spend a lot of time chasing each other, perhaps establishing pairs for the following spring. The drake teal perform mad dashes across the water and then dive under in a kind of belly flop. Quite often at this time shoveler ducks appear for short periods. The drakes are most attractive with bottle-green heads and bright chestnut sides.

With the onset of winter, the gulls arrive in strength. They feed at a nearby refuse tip by day, and for many of them this is a vital stopping-off place where they can have a drink and a wash. But some roost overnight, especially in the winter months. By far the commonest are black-headed gulls, with rather fewer common gulls. There are also the larger herring gulls, and even some greater black-backs, which are much the same size as Canada geese. On Christmas Day in 1981 400 of these massive gulls were feeding on scraps of household rubbish at the refuse tip with about 10,000 black-headed gulls, all of which made regular journeys to the sandpit for a wash; as the black-backs approach the lake, each lunges forward to take a drink just before it settles on the water.

As hard weather sets in, so other birds appear. Water rails, with their long red bills, may be seen skulking around the reedy margins and under the willow trees. So long as it remains unfrozen, the lake exerts a great attraction on water birds. A long-tailed duck, normally a bird of the open sea, stayed for a few weeks in November 1984, and on several occasions even divers have been seen. During a particularly cold spell in January 1985 a pair of red-breasted mergansers arrived on the adjacent lake, which had been stocked with fish for angling. The drake looked quite spectacular in the winter sunshine with his shaggy green cap and bright red bill. Cormorants, too, are occasional visitors there, no doubt because of the good fishing to be had. But soon the gulls and waterfowl will be flying north to their breeding grounds and, as the first pussywillow catkins burst and coltsfoot flowers appear, it will be time for the sand martins to return once again.

Below and opposite *Winter gathering of gulls at the sandpit.*

Familiarity with a particular place throughout the year provides a personal perspective on the natural world which cannot be gained in other ways. Simply being aware of the natural cycle and appreciating how your chosen spot figures in the wider scheme of things can transform even the most ordinary place. So it is with this sandpit. There must be many who see it and pass it by, unaware of its natural wonders. After all, it is a very unexceptional sandpit – not the kind of place that most people would wish to visit. But some do choose to go there. I know local residents who regard it as their own special place. They regularly walk the public footpath and enjoy the scene as it changes through the seasons, whether it is to see hoar frost on the old heads of hogweed or a winter sunset over the marshy wilderness. They may not be ardent naturalists but they take pleasure from watching the herons fishing, or from the occasional glimpse of a kingfisher flashing across the lake.

The sandpit described above is typical of many flooded sand and gravel quarries around the fringes of London. Each one, however mundane, has its own part to play, but some of the older pits, now full of reed and marsh, have become wonderful sanctuaries. Stocker's Lake in the Colne Valley near Rickmansworth is one of these. With its wooded islands and reedbeds it looks remarkably natural and supports an abundance of wildlife throughout the year. South of here is a string of gravel pits extending for several miles alongside the Grand Union Canal, the towpath of which provides a fine countryside walk on this western edge of London. Others in the Thames Valley near Heathrow are particularly good for winter wildfowl. In January 1986 the gravel pit at Wraysbury was one of the best places in London to see flocks of smew, winter visitors from Russia. A few miles east of here in the middle of the residential area of Staines and Feltham is Bedfont gravel pit, another notable place for wintering duck and very popular with wading birds in passage. On the east side of London is Ruxley gravel pit, in the valley of the Cray near Sidcup, which is now a nature reserve. Yet others occur in the low-lying land around Hornchurch and Upminster on the borders of Essex.

One of the strangest places associated with the gravel industry is Eastbrookend, a large area of unevenly restored gravel workings between Hornchurch and Dagenham. Here a multitude of ponds, marshes and shallow lagoons occur within a wide expanse of rough grassland dotted with willow and blackthorn scrub. Though the area is totally surrounded by the outer suburbs, there are wide vistas for over a mile along the valley of the Beam River and the unusual mixture of habitats provides a landscape unlike any other part of London. It is very good for wildlife too. Over fifty different sorts of birds are known to nest here, including waders such as redshank, lapwing and little ringed plovers. For them and many other ground-nesting birds, weekends during the nesting season are a difficult time in the face of numerous motorbike scramblers and horseriders. In winter herons can be seen fishing in the ponds and the rough grassland is full of snipe. Jack snipe too are present in small numbers most winters. Long-eared owls are reputed to roost here, and this is one of the more likely places in London to see that rare winter visitor from northern Europe the great grey shrike, preying on small birds among the thorn bushes.

Not so long ago there were plans for Eastbrookend to be turned into a golf course, but as the wildlife has become more widely appreciated it looks as though a large part will now be kept as a nature reserve – a prospect which applies increasingly to many of London's disused sand and gravel pits.

# ◆DERELICT INDUSTRIAL SITES AND RAILWAY SIDINGS◆

ONE OF MY FAVOURITE spots in central London is a patch of wasteland by the Thames next to Vauxhall Bridge. To some it is known as the Green Giant site because not long ago there was a proposal to build an enormous green skyscraper there. It is inaccessible to the public, but I have been fortunate to visit the plot which, at the time of writing, is still a green wilderness.

You have to stoop to pass through a tiny door, which is surely made for children, to enter a secret wild garden on the riverside. This place has been undisturbed since the Second World War. At one time there was a chemical factory here and I am told that some of the ground is still badly polluted. The remains of walls and flat slabs of concrete are still visible in places, but most of these vestiges of the past are now concealed under a mantle of vegetation. Low bushes of sallow, elder, hawthorn and buddleia are dotted about, and there are patches of bramble and bracken. Open areas are covered in drifts of colourful wasteland flowers, such as yellow melilot, michaelmas daisies and rosebay willowherb, with grassy banks of yorkshire fog, which are full of vetches and clover and strident with the sound of grasshoppers.

Wandering around this place on a warm summer's day is an education in wasteland ecology as well as being a delightful experience of London's natural history. Because of the rather poor soils which have developed on the rubble and other industrial debris, vigorous weeds have been held in check, and a host of less hardy plants have been able to establish themselves; quite small areas contain a considerable variety of species. In a typical open patch yarrow is abundant, along with the yellow heads of common sow-thistle and weld, or dyers rocket, which was once cultivated extensively for the production of yellow dye. Wild chamomile, an aromatic flower resembling the scentless mayweed, is also found; this plant is still used in the production of oil of chamomile. Tiny mauve flowers of the small toadflax can be found among the creeping stems of the small pink field bindweed. Coltsfoot leaves cover piles of stony spoil and, in more open spots, ribwort plantain grows alongside two kinds of sorrel, which, though insignificant as flowers, are all-important as the food plant of the small copper butterfly. Even gypsywort occurs here, in places which are strangely dry for such a water-loving plant. Red clover and yellow hop trefoil cover the ground, bringing vital nitrogen to the slowly developing soil.

Patches of taller plants include some of the commonest of London's wasteland flowers. Red-stemmed mugwort, and Canadian fleabane with its numerous tiny flowers, both proliferate. Wormwood, a near relative of the mugwort, which has long been cultivated around London for use as a herbal remedy, can also be found – as can the tall heads of evening primrose, mallow, teasel and even a magnificent Scotch thistle. At times in July, when the melilot is in flower, the whole place seems to be a sea of yellow. Later it turns to red as rosebay willowherb takes its turn, giving way to drifts of pale blue michaelmas daisies in the autumn.

Even the walls have their specialities. Wall rocket grows on many of the surviving fragments of masonry and clumps of the beautiful red pellitory-of-the-wall are rooted in the brickwork of the river wall, where it grows well out of the wind. In some places woody nightshade climbs among the tangle of vegetation and some of the bushes are white with trumpets of calystegia. In others, there are a few potato plants, a legacy of the gypsy encampment which occupied the site two years ago.

Most of the plants here originated as windborne seeds. A single plant of rosebay willowherb, for example, may produce eighty thousand seeds, sow thistles about half that number. Each evening primrose plant can produce up to thirty thousand seeds, which may survive up to forty years before germinating. Seeds of others, such as the bramble, have arrived in other ways, possibly dropped by birds. Once established, the bramble, as every gardener knows, has a great ability to spread. Some of the concrete slabs are covered in long shoots of the plant; each one is looking for footholds in this barren territory, putting roots down in any crack it finds. It seems that there has been no available source of tree seeds, otherwise the place would surely have been colonised by sycamore and ash saplings within the past forty years.

*Bramble seeking a foothold in concrete.* David Goode

Opposite *Buddleia growing on a disused warehouse.*

When I visited this green wilderness late in August, it was humming with insects. One small patch of michaelmas daisies was attracting dozens of bees, flies and butterflies. Honeybees were there in quantity, along with several kinds of hover fly and a number of brightly coloured flies. One was an iridescent-green soldier fly and there were also several small black and red flies called *Eryothryx rufomaculata*, which are parasitic on moths. The butterflies clustering on the flower heads included small tortoiseshell, red admiral and meadow brown. On the other flowers nearby were small skippers and the rarer Essex skipper, which is actually quite abundant in the London area. Common blue butterflies sat on the clover and small whites on wall rocket. As usual, buddleia flowers were a great attraction, not only to butterflies but also to honey bees and red-tailed bumblebees. On ragwort there were black and yellow striped caterpillars of the cinnabar moth. Snails were everywhere. Song thrushes would have had a field day, but the only birds I saw were goldfinches on the thistle heads.

Despite the noise of planes flying over central London on the way to Heathrow, trains on the nearby overhead line at Vauxhall, and the roar of traffic every time the lights changed just beyond the advertisement hoardings, I could hear the ceaseless chirping of grasshoppers and the call of black-headed gulls as they passed along the river.

For many Londoners the sight of rosebay willowherb is a grim reminder of the wartime blitz, when it covered the bomb sites in a blaze of red. The colonisation of these bomb sites was mainly accomplished by a group of plants with windborne seeds, of which rosebay was perhaps the most spectacular. But Oxford ragwort and Canadian fleabane also covered vast tracts of central London, together with dandelion, spear thistle, gallant soldiers, two kinds of groundsel and coltsfoot. Four of these were introduced species which had not been particularly abundant previously and were suddenly able to spread into this newly created habitat. Oxford ragwort was one; it first became naturalised in Britain as an escape from cultivation at the Oxford Botanic Gardens in the late eighteenth century. In its native Sicily it grows on the soils derived from volcanic ash on Mount Etna and is obviously well designed to cope with rapid colonisation of new areas. These original colonisers were gradually replaced by open grassland and tall herbs, as has happened at the Green Giant site. Many other sites were rapidly colonised by buddleia – for example, a small patch of land among buildings near Borough Market in Bermondsey is almost entirely covered in buddleia. Other bomb sites have gradually been colonised by sycamore, and even ash, where a seed source has been available.

Just off Ludgate Hill is small bomb site now used as a carpark, where yellow stonecrop grows on the concrete of an old chimney breast and fronds of bracken sprout from the grate. Evening primrose flowers on top of the brickwork and blackbirds nest in beautifully tiled alcoves in the walls. Bluetits nest in the remains of a drainpipe and in recent years dunnocks have bred amid the tangle of climbing knotweed.

Even quite small bomb sites can hold surprises. One of the oddest I have come across is a small patch of land surrounded by corrugated iron and advertisement hoardings by a busy road in the middle of Bermondsey. Here bogbean grows in the flooded basement of a bombed-out building. When I was last there, a pair of grey wagtails was nesting and red darter dragonflies were laying eggs in the small pond.

Mention derelict land in London and for many people it is the docks which spring to mind. Acres of abandoned wharves and goods yards are now colonised by a great variety of wasteland plants. Plenty of examples can be seen along the Thames downstream of Tower Bridge. Some of the best for wildlife are the wharves along Deptford Strand and across the river at Klein's Wharf on the Isle of Dogs. Here, in addition to the usual mixture of mugwort, rocket and melilot, you can find warty cabbage, treacle mustard, wild parsnip and giant hogweed growing among the derelict bollards and capstans of the quays. Kestrels nest in some of the disused warehouses and cormorants can often be seen perching on jetties along this stretch of the river.

Many of the plants growing on old wharves and jetties have been brought in from abroad as a result of the dockland trade. A nice example was an arctic rock cress which grew for several years by the gasworks at Bromley-by-Bow on a pile of iron ore which had come from Scandinavia.

*Blackbirds and dunnocks nest in this bombsite by Ludgate Hill and the walls have been colonised by stonecrop and evening primrose.*

*Mallard's nest in a reed bed near Deptford Wharf.*

*Ferns and buddleia growing on the old dock walls at St Katherine's Dock.*

*Natural window boxes; an alien rocket growing on a disused warehouse near Tower Bridge.*

Further down the river at Canning Town is a large area of disused wharves, railway yards and other derelict land beside Bow Creek. Such is the variety of habitats developed here that stonechats, meadow pipits, grey wagtails and pheasants all find it suitable for breeding. Even red-legged partridge have been seen, and both herons and kingfishers are known to fish along the ditches.

Other patches of derelict land along the Thames which are notable for their wildlife include the disused gasworks land at Beckton and parts of Barking level, where marsh orchids grow on ash dumps from the local power station. Another strange wilderness can be seen south of the river near Tripcock Ness, where acres of willow and elder bushes grow among the disused buildings and tramways of the old Woolwich Arsenal.

Alongside the Old Kent Road in Bermondsey, about one mile from Guy's Hospital, is a disused goods station called the Bricklayer's Arms. After a brief spell as a passenger terminal when it was first opened in 1844, the station was turned over to goods traffic, and for over a hundred years it was a busy coalyard and goods depot catering for local industries. In post war years its importance gradually declined and, in 1962, the railway sheds were closed. The South Eastern Railway Company's fine Victorian stables for the dray horses can still be seen by the bridge on St James's Road. Horses of a different kind are kept there now – for inner-city horseriding.

*The small copper, one of the more attractive butterflies of wasteland sites in London.* David Goode
Left *Buddleia bushes growing on disused railway tracks at the Bricklayer's Arms goods-yard in Southwark.* David Goode

Since the goods yard closed it has become wild and is now rarely frequented. Most of the tracks were left for many years and only removed in the early 1980s; some still remain. Over this period plants have grown up between the sleepers and on the embankments, creating new habitats for wildlife. One of the most fascinating parts of the yard is the area of railway tracks and banks along the north side by St Augustine's Church. Below the bridge on St James's Road is a jungle of buddleia bushes festooned in calystegia, with tall beds of bracken all around. Beyond, the scrub extends along the old sidings for more than a quarter of a mile, with thickets of willow, sycamore and elder with patches of birch on the banks near Galley Wall Road. There are bramble patches too, and clumps of the pernicious Japanese knotweed. Bladder senna has established itself in places, and occasional bushes of gorse, broom and even the Duke of Argyle's tea plant can be found. Around the edges of the scrub are tangles of bright pink everlasting pea, sometimes mixed with old man's beard, a plant normally associated with chalky soils. Several other plants common to calcareous regions also occur, including the tall yellow spikes of wild mignonette. Blue fleabane and pale toadflax also occur in the open grassy areas. Either some chalky soil has been dumped here in the past or these plants for some reason find the rather unusual conditions to their liking.

Among the clinker and ballast of the old railway tracks there is now a medley of flowers and insects. Old man's beard twines around the iron shoes and rails, spreading out to create a mat of beautiful downy fruits. In the bare ballast pale yellow flowers of toadflax grow in profusion. Here too are yarrow, black medic, red clover and a variety of yellow 'composites', including common cat's ear and hawkweed oxtongue. Tall spikes of evening primrose adorn the remains of an old railway junction by the derelict signal-box, where saplings of buddleia and birch are rapidly taking over. Sneezewort, horseradish and narrow-leaved pepperwort grow on the railway too, and in places there are primroses and St John's wort. Some of the early colonisers can still be found, especially fireweed, goldenrod, Canadian fleabane and coltsfoot.

With primroses and coltsfoot early in the year, and banks of michaelmas daisies in the autumn, the yard is rarely without an attractive display of flowers. Throughout the summer there are plenty of butterflies too. On a warm day in late August there were 9 different kinds. Meadow browns were particularly abundant in the open grassy places where red clover was in flower. Here also were common blue, small heath and the delightful small copper. Among the many small skippers, there were a few Essex skippers. Even a wall and painted lady were feeding along the railway track, and neighbouring buddleia bushes were covered in small tortoiseshells with occasional red admirals and painted ladies. Somewhere in the scrub a willow warbler was calling, a temporary visitor on its way south. A pair of kestrels made a lot of noise chasing from post to post across the old sidings and over nearby rooftops; it is probably good hunting for them, with plenty of beetles and voles. In winter flocks of meadow pipits, skylarks and finches forage between the railway tracks.

All around this wild area are the rooftops of Bermondsey. Tower blocks of flats, church steeples and gas holders rise above the streets of terraced houses with their endless rows of chimneypots. A little further afield is the distinctive tower of Guy's Hospital and the twin turrets of Tower Bridge. The Bricklayer's Arms is the wild city at its best.

◆

Over in west London, not far from Heathrow airport, another disused railway siding is fast reverting to the wild. This is Feltham marshalling yard, which extends for over a mile beside the railway running along the southern edge of Hounslow Heath. This huge area of sidings was built on a wide embankment across the shallow valley of the River Crane, which now flows underneath it in a culvert. The yard was closed in 1968, since when it has rapidly been colonised by a great variety of plants, many of which may have been introduced to the area by the trains themselves.

*A rich array of wild flowers forming a mature wasteland plant community at Feltham marshalling yards.*
David Goode

All the railway tracks have long since gone, to be replaced by a wilderness of birch and willow thickets and open patches full of flowers. Scrub has developed more quickly here than at the Bricklayer's Arms, perhaps because it is further from central London and has benefited from local sources of seed. Large areas are colonised by birch, whitebeam, elder, hawthorn – and even occasional bushes of bladder senna, which has attractive yellow pea flowers and large swollen pods. This plant was first introduced to Britain from North Africa in the sixteenth century and, because it can thrive in even the poorest soils, has often been planted in gardens. Like its close relative the laburnum, its seeds are poisonous, but the flowers are a valuable source of nectar for bees. In the London area it has spread along railway banks remarkably effectively and I have even seen it growing in a disused coalyard at the back of St Pancras station.

The marshalling yards are a good place to pick blackberries. Bramble patches abound. There are also beautiful little upright bushes of dogrose. Among the thickets are open areas, resembling hayfields that have not produced a very good crop of grass. They are full of colourful flowers. Where the vegetation is cropped short by rabbits, there are clovers and trefoils, including the hare's-foot clover and meadow vetching. Common storksbill and pale toadflax occur here, along with salad burnet – not the same plant as found on the downs, but a variety which used to be grown as a fodder crop and has now become naturalised. In rougher areas there are taller flowers of yarrow, field scabious, viper's bugloss, wild mignonette, black knapweed and crow garlic. Fifteen different sorts of grass grow in this rather sparse vegetation, including the lesser cat's tail and silvery hair grass. One of the loveliest flowers to be found here is the sky-blue wild chicory.

Twenty-three different kinds of butterfly are regularly seen here. The open grassy areas provide an ideal habitat for the small copper, meadow brown, small heath and skippers. Others include the grayling, orange tip and comma. In one area, glades of mature trees support a colony of speckled wood butterflies. In the summer the old yards are rich in insect life and have become a popular haunt of London's entomologists – as well as with local people, who have come to regard this as an unofficial open space. Grey wagtails and kingfishers can be seen from the footpath by the River Crane and in the autumn the grasslands are alive with dancing flocks of linnets and goldfinches.

Smaller plots of disused railway land are dotted all around the capital and some are now very well disguised. Many of those abandoned only 40 years ago are today covered in birch woodland. A five-acre plot between the railways at Gunnersbury in Chiswick, used for allotment gardens in the 1930s, is now a mature wood of birch and willow. Birch has also invaded the disused branch line to Alexandra Palace in Haringey, now known as the Parkland Walk, covering the banks and forming a small piece of woodland around the old Highgate station. A former group of railway sidings at Streatham Vale must now rank as the biggest self-sown birch wood in the built-up parts of inner London. A smaller railside strip of about three acres along Shakespeare Road in Brixton is notable for its profusion of mosses and lichens growing on the acidic surface of the old railway tracks, and in 1985 there was great excitement when bee orchids were found growing here.

Not far from where the London to Gatwick railway cuts through the chalk, what used to be a small gravelly carpark is now covered in a most attractive array of plants, reminiscent of an herbaceous border. It is at its best in late July, when the flat central area is covered in a swathe of St John's wort, forming a continuous golden-yellow canopy about eighteen inches high. Down among the stems are tiny spikes of pink-headed centaury and mauve sneezewort. The ground itself is covered in mosses and fairy flax, with creeping strands of scarlet pimpernel and yellow bird's-foot trefoil. Protruding from the canopy of St John's wort are numerous tall thin spikes of wild mignonette, giving the appearance of a stand of cactus plants. All around the edge is a bank of tall flowers growing in more fertile soil. Mullein grows to a height of four feet, with clusters of bright yellow flowers, and there is evening primrose too, against a background of tall purple thistles, pink heads of codlins and cream and huge white garden daisies. It has all the appearance of a well-planned garden, though, sadly, lasts for only a few weeks each year.

In a nearby valley the railway from Croydon to Woldingham crosses a viaduct through disused chalk quarries at Riddlesdown. This is a magnificent place, with towering cliffs of chalk and a wonderful array of chalkland flowers and insects which have recolonised the old workings. One of its special features is a thriving colony of jackdaws which nest in the quarry face and feed on the downland turf above. I could sit and watch their antics for hours, they are such delightful birds. To some people this is just another piece of derelict land, but for many who walk the footpaths of Riddlesdown the quarry is very special.

# ◆ CEMETERIES ◆

AS I WALKED THROUGH the City one day, beneath the towering glass and concrete office blocks of its financial institutions, the total absence of greenery made me wonder where the nearest piece of woodland might be found. The answer, so far as genuine woodland is concerned, must be Ken Wood, over five miles away at Hampstead. But the ordnance survey map shows a small patch of woodland, less than half that distance from the City, in Tower Hamlets; it is also marked as a cemetery. The map is quite correct, for this is in fact a wooded cemetery. There are others like it at Abney Park in Stoke Newington, Nunhead near Camberwell and the famous old cemetery at Highgate. They are all town woodlands of a most unusual kind, with a fascinating history.

---

*Opposite A colourful collection of wild flowers on this patch of disused land by the railway south of Purley includes St John's wort, wild mignonette, mullein and evening primrose. David Goode*

During the early years of the nineteenth century the population of London suddenly started to increase dramatically. Previously its growth had been fairly gradual, but between 1800 and 1830 it rose from 856,000 to one and half million, eventually bringing to a head a problem which had already been developing for some time: where to bury the dead.

London's small churchyards could no longer cope. After all, they were simply the graveyards of village churches, which had now been overtaken by London, where at one time a few hundred graves would have sufficed. Many were already filled to capacity with bodies several deep. The shallow, overcrowded graves of these city burial grounds became a public scandal. Some way had to be found to provide for upwards of 52,000 burials a year. So, during the 1830s, Parliament gave consent for several large new cemeteries to be developed. Naturally enough, attention was focused on suitable places in the countryside surrounding London where land was readily available.

Kensal Green Cemetery was the first to be opened following an Act of Parliament in 1832 which allowed for establishing a general cemetery for interment of the dead in the neighbourhood of the metropolis. Others quickly followed. New companies sprang into life to develop and run cemeteries. When Queen Victoria came to the throne a spate of new burial grounds was being planned, and by 1841 at least seven were operating all around London. Kensal Green, Highgate, Abney Park, Tower Hamlets, Nunhead, Norwood and Brompton form a ring which has a curious symmetry about it. Most of them are situated between four and five miles from Charing Cross, illustrating the limited extent of London's built-up area at that time, since all were developed in open countryside. When the cemetery there was developed, Kensal Green was no more than a hamlet amid small fields and waterlogged pastures beside the Grand Union Canal a couple of miles from the Paddington basin. Similarly, Highgate cemetery, opened in 1839, was built in the extensive grounds of a former country mansion on the slopes of Highgate Hill overlooking fields to the south. Even Tower Hamlets Cemetery was surrounded by farmland beyond Mile End when it was opened in 1840.

The concept of large cemeteries was relatively new, and the layout of Kensal Green followed the formal landscape design of the recently completed Père Lachais Cemetery outside Paris. Early pictures of Kensal Green show tree-lined avenues and large areas of neatly trimmed lawn. But the Victorian cemetery companies were in competition with each other. Their cemeteries had to be attractive places where people would want to be buried, and it was not long before some of them were designed along less formal lines. More intricate landscapes of winding paths and shrubberies were created. Exotic trees and shrubs were planted by the thousand. Evergreens and weeping specimen trees contributed to a rather special atmosphere of peace and tranquillity, described by some 'as a sense of pleasing melancholy'.

Cypress, cedar, swamp cyprus, false acacia, Indian bean tree, weeping ash, ginkgo and monkey puzzle trees were planted, along with a host of ornamental shrubs; many of these were evergreens such as box, holly, privet and laurel, but there were plenty of other more attractive species too. At Abney Park the cemetery was even planned as an arboretum with 2500 varieties of trees and shrubs and over 1000 varieties of rose bushes.

Opposite *Angel at Nunhead Cemetery*

The new cemeteries provided an excuse for Victorian extravagance on a grand scale. Elaborate tombs, monuments and catacombs became the order of the day, and nowhere were they developed to better effect than at the old Highgate Cemetery. Here the centrepiece was an extraordinary series of ornately decorated vaults forming sunken pathways built into the hill itself. These were entered through an imposing Egyptian-style archway leading to the 'Circle of Lebanon', a sunken lane, lined with rows of vaults, surrounding an ancient cedar tree. The whole edifice created an aura of antiquity which no doubt pandered to the fashion of the times.

Highgate Cemetery certainly became a very fashionable place to be buried. In fact, all these early Victorian cemeteries developed into profitable businesses, particularly after the closure of the City burial grounds in 1852. In their heyday they produced a considerable income and the companies were able to employ dozens of gardeners to look after the grounds. At one time 28 gardeners were employed at Highgate alone. By then, the majority of the trees had matured and the cemetery had turned into a woodland; with all the paths and monuments, it needed many hands to keep it in order.

Unfortunately for the cemetery companies, their income dwindled as the years went by, simply because the amount of land available for burials was gradually used up. The number of bodies crammed into some of these cemeteries is astonishing. According to Mrs Holmes, who wrote about London's burial grounds in 1896, a total of 247,000 bodies were interred within the 27 acres of Tower Hamlets Cemetery by 1889. As space became more restricted, the companies resorted to burials along the paths and rides, even removing some of the fine specimen trees to make room for more graves.

At the same time the need for maintenance increased. With mature trees producing seedlings in profusion a continuous battle began to stem the tide of encroaching trees and shrubs. It was only a matter of time before some of the cemeteries reached crisis point. In some cases it happened remarkably quickly. It seems from Mrs Holmes's description that, as early as 1896, large parts of Tower Hamlets Cemetery were becoming sadly neglected:

> Still in use and open daily, a regular ocean of tombstones, many of which are lying about apparently uncared for and unclaimed; in fact most of the graves except those at the edges of the walks look utterly neglected and parts of the ground are very untidy.

The two world wars seem to have been crucial factors in the process of dereliction. With no gardeners available, vegetation spread unchecked. The last war, in particular, was a turning point for several of these cemeteries, including Highgate, Nunhead and Abney Park, since when they have fallen into decay. In other cases the battle is still going on. A recent account of Kensal Green Cemetery mentions that income from the few burials that still take place there is sufficient only to ensure that basic maintenance is carried out, and the reduced workforce fight a rearguard action against the advancing vegetation.

Highgate, Nunhead, Abney Park and Tower Hamlets are now wild places where nature has taken over among the gravestones and monuments. Marble and granite are wreathed in ivy, and winding paths disappear in thickets of sycamore saplings. Buddleia grows out of the stonework and cow parsley covers the open rides. Though still full of Victorian graves and vaults, these cemeteries are now town woodlands and each has its own particular wildlife specialities.

◆

*Nunhead Cemetery is one of several Victorian cemeteries which are now overgrown and have turned to woodland. This is now one of the largest pieces of woodland close to the centre of London.*

In postwar years large parts of Tower Hamlets Cemetery were covered by dense thickets of sycamore, with innumerable thin green saplings growing up between the serried ranks of graves. Acres of stonework, and trees too, became covered in a green blanket of ivy. Woodland flowers were able to grow alongside the paths and in the more open glades. Despite its urban setting, over a hundred different species of plants have been found in this cemetery. Foxgloves, red campion, herb robert and woody nightshade may not seem particularly unusual, but in the context of London's East End this self-sown woodland is remarkable.

The birdlife of this cemetery is what you might expect of a fairly wild city park. Common birds of suburban gardens are there in abundance, especially wrens, robins, dunnocks and blackbirds. There are plenty of woodpigeons too, and it is thought that greenfinches, blackcaps and long-tailed tits all nest. Tawny owls can often be heard

hooting and kestrels regularly hunt over the cemetery, though the only small mammal
in any abundance seems to be the nocturnal woodmouse. Magpies, jays and carrion
crows are all in residence, and occasionally a pied woodpecker has been seen. In the
summer of 1985 a cuckoo spent a month in the cemetery, calling in vain, for it seems
that there was no mate within earshot.

At times speckled wood butterflies flicker among the trees and this cemetery is a
favoured location for the holly blue. This delightful little pale lilac butterfly seems to
cope with the urban environment better than many, perhaps because it is largely
dependent on holly and ivy for its food. It can often be seen on the wing in May, when
it lays eggs on holly flowers. Later in the year a second batch of butterflies uses ivy,
laying eggs on the developing flower buds in preparation for their pupae to pass the
winter attached to the plant's foliage.

◆

*A wilderness of ivy-covered tombstones at Nunhead Cemetery in winter. The mixture of woodland and
open glades provides ideal conditions for a nature reserve.*

*Headstones and monuments among sycamore saplings at Nunhead.* David Goode

Nunhead Cemetery has a very different feel. Covering over sixty acres, it is much larger, and substantial parts are still quite open, with grassy glades and clumps of bushes among the tombs. Large areas have turned to mature woodlands but there is a greater variety of trees here than at Tower Hamlets. Patches of dense sycamore occur but ash, birch, elm and even elder and aspen have all established themselves by natural colonisation. Some magnificent specimen trees can still be seen, including ash, turkey oak, cypress and limes. There is even a ginkgo, sadly smothered in ivy and hemmed in by sycamores.

The rough grassland between the tombs and monuments is full of flowers. Ox-eye daisies and blue meadow cranesbills grow alongside hardheads and wild camomile. Pink cups of field bindweed trail over the gravestones, and in the short cropped turf where rabbits graze there is self heal and bird's-foot trefoil. During the summer months, the glades are full of common field grasshoppers. There is also a great variety of butterflies. In addition to the usual meadow brown and skippers, small copper and brimstone are frequent. I remember noticing clouded yellows here too during their last influx into Britain in 1983. Large numbers of speckled wood butterflies can be seen along the woodland paths. This part of the cemetery has a strong feel of real woodland about it, enhanced perhaps by the song of chiffchaffs from the treetops. Several can be heard singing in different parts of the cemetery; it is perhaps the nearest place to the centre of London where these woodland warblers breed. Along the woodland paths bluebells and creeping jenny grow among dog's mercury and ground elder. It has been estimated that about sixty pairs of wrens nest in the cemetery; there are certainly plenty of holes for them to choose from.

Abney Park Cemetery in Stoke Newington has many similarities to Nunhead, though it lacks such a large area of mature woodland. Here again there are pied woodpeckers and tawny owls. Even stockdoves nest in the pollarded poplars which are a distinctive feature of the place. In May there is a spectacular dawn chorus with the song of blackcaps, willow warblers and chiffchaffs mingling with that of countless robins, dunnocks and thrushes. With its spinneys of birch and grotesque old poplars sprouting out of the ornate headstones, Abney Park is a very beautiful place.

All the old cemeteries contain interesting plants of one kind or another. Pellitory-of-the-wall is abundant in Brompton Cemetery, where wall lettuce can also be found. Six species of fern grow in Kensal Green Cemetery, including hart's tongue, black spleenwort and even maidenhair spleenwort. This cemetery is remarkably rich in plant life. A recent survey identified 320 species some of which must have persisted from the time before the site was developed as a cemetery. Bluebells, wood anemones and primroses suggest that coppice woodland once prevailed. Wild arum, guelder rose and old man's beard probably grew along hedgerows. More surprising is the presence of meadowsweet, sneezewort, hoary ragwort and great burnet, all plants typical of wet meadows. A few years ago a patch of several hundred green-winged orchids was discovered in the New Battersea Cemetery, where they had probably survived from earlier grassland. Unfortunately they have since disappeared as a result of rather too intensive a mowing regime in what is still an active cemetery.

The overgrown cemeteries of Nunhead, Tower Hamlets and Abney Park have all been taken into public ownership. But what of Highgate? The old cemetery at Highgate is a must for any explorer of London's natural history. Now looked after by the Friends of Highgate Cemetery (having been acquired in 1981 from the cemetery company for £50), it is open regularly to visitors and is without doubt one of the wonders of London. Its history was well described in 1984 in a book about the cemetery by Felix Barber and John Gay.

*Nunhead cemetery in winter.* NCW

A winding path leads gently up the hill from the entrance past ivy-covered tombs and monuments almost hidden among the trees. The wooded slopes create a sense of intimacy, heightened by the layout of the paths. Holly, yew and privet grow in profusion and everywhere, it seems, there are the thin green stems of sycamore, invading every tomb. When I was last there a goldcrest sang from the depths of a yew tree by an open grassy circle near the foot of the cemetery. There was a distinct smell of fox, and I'm told that foxes have been resident for many years. No doubt they are unmolested nowadays, but there was apparently a foxhunt in the cemetery in 1900! I caught another whiff of fox in the Egyptian Avenue. This part of the cemetery is an extraordinary sight, with festoons of ivy hanging over the ornate stonework of the vaults and trees sprouting out of the stonework above. It feels as if one is walking into a lost city which has long ago been overtaken by the jungle. Ferns and buddleia sprout from cracks in the stonework and high above are the branches of a 300-year-old cedar which forms the centrepiece of the Circle of Lebanon.

From the highest point of the cemetery it is possible to look southwards to the City and enjoy one of the finest views in the whole of London.

# ◆ PARKS ◆

ONE OF MY FAVOURITE haunts in central London is the bridge over the lake in St James's Park. A lunchtime visit is always worthwhile, for one never knows what might be seen. I remember one particular occasion very vividly. It was a winter's day and there were hundreds of black-headed gulls in the park making the most of a steady supply of food from visitors like myself. As I stood on the bridge, the birds would swoop in low, hover briefly, and then snatch a piece of bread from my outstretched hand. When there were few people about, some even landed on the rail of the bridge and stood in a row waiting to be fed. The more daring would take food from my hand.

I overheard a young mother and her child watching the ducks below us. 'Just look at that, they are swimming right under the water,' she said, and her daughter squealed with delight as a smart black and white tufted duck suddenly popped up to the surface with water running off its back in silver droplets. Standing by them was a man who rarely misses a lunchtime visit. He was throwing grain into the water from a plastic carrier bag, causing turmoil below. Every handful of food produced a mad rush of jostling ducks and coot. As the grain sank, so the tufties dived after it. The water was so clear that you could see them dashing about on the muddy bottom of the lake snapping up the food. Meanwhile the coot squabbled over the pickings left on the surface.

Nearby an elderly man was feeding sparrows. He gave some birdseed to the little girl and told her to hold her hand up high. Immediately she had a cluster of sparrows on her hand pecking away at the seed. But then she suddenly found a pigeon perched on her arm and another on her head, and that of course was too much. They all laughed and her mother said, 'Isn't it amazing, here we are in the centre of London and there is all this!'

At that moment everything suddenly took to the air. Pigeons flew in tight flocks, sweeping low over the bridge, giving everyone a fright. Sparrows took refuge in nearby bushes and even the ducks moved away to huddle in the middle of the lake. The gulls rose into the sky, where they circled round, calling incessantly. The reason for all the commotion was a kestrel hovering momentarily overhead; it drifted off in the direction of Buckingham Palace gardens and as it went I heard it call once or twice, a sharp kek-kek-kek, but then its voice was drowned by the noise of a jumbo jet lumbering over London on its way to Heathrow.

*Feeding ducks and sparrows is a popular pastime in St James's Park. Some of the captive bred ducks, including this goldeneye, are very attractive.* David Goode

*St James's Park – the finest nature reserve in central London.*

I am not alone in enjoying the wildlife of St James's Park. A regular succession of 'bird feeders' bring food for the sparrows and ducks. Some spend so much time in the park that they can recognise individual birds. One man comes up by train from the Sussex coast nearly every weekend bringing a couple of loaves and several pounds of birdseed. He will spend virtually the whole day in the park. Most of these regulars are elderly men or women who find genuine enjoyment in their personal contact with the birds. They meet a lot of people too. One man makes friends with American tourists who like to have their photos taken with a handful of cockney sparrows. He now has a huge collection of postcards from all over the States thanking him for 'his' birds. For some it was apparently the highlight of their trip! Feeding the sparrows is now such a popular ritual that the park staff have even found people selling birdseed to the tourists.

Regular visitors get to know a lot about the habits of the birds. Charles Handley, who comes to the park most days from Dulwich, looks forward each year to the time when the sparrows bring their newly fledged brood from their nests in the nearby lamp posts on the Mall. Then he has a whole family of baby sparrows being fed by their mother in the palm of his hand. He tells me that he has been feeding sparrows in his garden for seventy years and never managed to get them on his hand. It seems they are too suspicious of cats in suburban gardens, but have little to fear in St James's. The sparrows of St James's know one of the regulars so well that as soon as he appears they fly straight onto his hat, or perch on his shoulders, waiting to be fed. He lives near Caxton Hall and in the cold weather of January 1985 noticed that all the sparrows roosted at night in the nearby tube station. Another, recently retired visitor, spends a lot of time in the park feeding them on madeira cake. During the summer months she was most concerned about the behaviour of the pelicans, which seemed to have developed a mid-morning habit of swimming up to the bridge for duckling snack.

One person who knows the wild birds here better than most is Audley Gosling, who has been visiting the park regularly for the past eight years and regards it as the finest bird laboratory in the world. His particular interest is the gulls. I think he looks forward to the annual return of the black-headed gulls with the same sense of expectation that I feel for swifts; but he knows the individual birds much more intimately. In recent years he has kept a record of all the birds which were ringed abroad, noting the times when each bird first arrives and when he last sees it. Using binoculars, he identifies individuals from the numbered rings on their legs.

It is now well known that many of the gulls wintering in London come from the Baltic, but it must be exciting to see particular birds return, and know that since you last saw them in the park in early March they have been to a nesting colony in some Lithuanian marsh. Some of the birds which arrive back early in July are from Lithuania, Estonia and East Germany; others may be from Holland and Belgium. The results of Gosling's studies so far confirm that these birds return to the same place each winter from their breeding grounds around the Baltic. One bird ringed in Norway in 1977 has spent each of the past three winters in the park and was also seen there in 1980. In the same way that individual commuters can be seen day after day on the same spot on the platform waiting for the eight-fifteen, so some gulls are attached to particular places. One bird spends the whole winter feeding just outside the restaurant in the park. Others stay for a few months and then move elsewhere, every winter. The oldest gull recorded in this study is one ringed in Prague in 1971, which was nearly 16 years old when last seen.

Audley Gosling's other great love is taming the birds. He started three years ago with woodpigeons. By feeding them regularly and gradually getting them to come closer, he eventually had them eating out of his hands. For two months they wouldn't go to anyone else and he was the envy of all the other 'bird feeders'. But eventually they did take to other people and now some of the woodpigeons will go to anyone with food; they will even let you stroke them. But if Audley appears they make a beeline for him. He tried some experiments to find out how they recognised him: wearing different clothes and carrying a different bag, even varying his route through the park – but all to no avail. They still knew who he was immediately – perhaps it was from his distinctive face or the way he walked. He also found that some of these woodies remembered him even after he had been away for up to four months, and would fly straight to his hand.

Food seems to be the clue to taming such birds, and not just during hard weather. In summer, when the birds are feeding young, the need may be as great. Audley established a remarkable relationship with one mallard duck completely by accident. She was incubating eggs at the time and she came begging for food in a fairly frantic manner. He fed her on grain, which is ideal for ducks, and from that moment she never forgot. Whenever she saw him coming, she would fly from the lake and land at his feet, often following him for long walks through the park. Another bird that he tamed in St James's Park was a carrion crow. As well as eating out of his hand, it would even pick him out in a crowd and drop down for food, to the astonishment of those nearby.

The collection of waterfowl managed by the Royal Parks staff is one of the most attractive features of St James's Park. The birds include exotic species such as pelicans, black swans, Carolina wood ducks and red-crested pochards; but there are plenty of native British species too. The park is a fine place to see shoveler, pintail, gadwall and goldeneye at close quarters, as well as brent and barnacle geese and the commoner ducks such as pochard and tufties. At times when the lake is frozen, the concentration of waterfowl in patches of water by the restaurant presents a magnificent spectacle, with a great variety of colours among the ducks, geese and swans.

One feature of this park which makes it particularly hospitable to wildfowl is the narrow border of grass which surrounds the lake, turning it into a kind of nature reserve, where people can look but cannot go. Some might call the area a waterfowl park; it has also been described as an outdoor aviary.

Malcolm Kerr, the birdkeeper for the Royal Parks – aptly called by some 'the duck man' – is responsible for the waterfowl of the central London parks, including those in the gardens of Buckingham Palace. Few people realise that hidden in the trees of Duck Island by Horseguards Parade is a remarkable establishment for rearing waterfowl. This island sanctuary, which Malcolm supervises, is a world apart from the corridors of power in the Foreign Office just across the road. Both have mandarins, but their territories are very different. Here among the trees are two hundred nestboxes for ducks, buildings housing an incubator room and pens for rearing ducklings and goslings. There are special underground nestboxes resembling rabbit burrows for shelduck, and boxes attached to trees to cater for mandarins and Carolina ducks. Boxes of all shapes and sizes dotted round the island provide homes for mallard, tufted ducks, pochard, shoveler and goldeneye. Eggs are collected and 'brought on' in incubators and the ducklings are reared for the first few weeks in pens before being released onto the lake. This method of maintaining or increasing the duck population is cheaper than buying in new stocks.

Malcolm Kerr puts a lot of effort into encouraging new species to nest, trying out nestboxes in a variety of places. One of his recent successes has been the goldeneye duck; in 1985, 4 pairs produced 12 young. Black swans are another triumph. It took eight years to establish their breeding; now he supplies black swans to other Royal Parks around London, including Windsor.

---

Opposite *Ornamental wildfowl and truly wild birds are all mixed together during the winter months in St James's Park*. David Goode

Today only the more exotic waterfowl are pinioned; the majority are allowed to develop as free-flying birds. Many mallard and tufted ducks are left to rear broods by themselves and several pairs nest on the island at the end of the lake by Buckingham Palace. Some of the other park birds are a nuisance: pelicans are known to eat young diving ducks, and coots take a lot of eggs and prey on chicks. The coot population of St James's is extraordinary; about 30 pairs now nest each year and, perhaps because there is no shortage of food, they have become colonial in their habits, quite unlike coot in more natural situations, which tend to be very aggressive towards one another. Herring gulls nesting on the nearby rooftops also prey on mallard ducklings and young coot. Malcolm told me that he had problems with a fox a couple of years ago, which came over from Holland Park each night. The police used to see it going through the subway at Hyde Park Corner into Green Park and then across the road by the palace into St James's. But the birds on Duck Island are reasonably safe from such intruders, and no doubt it helps if young ducklings are kept in pens for their first few weeks.

The newly hatched ducklings are a delight. One June day in the hatchery there was an assortment of tiny mallard, pochard, tufties and shoveler, their plumage a beautiful mixture of browns and yellows. Day-old shovelers were already quite distinctive, with their elongated bills and fluffy down. There were smartly striped ducklings of shelduck too; only three inches high, they were already posturing in the manner of the adult birds, with necks bent low and bills lifted to ward off intruders.

As I walked across the park that same morning, tufted ducks were shepherding flotillas of tiny offspring around the lake. The day-old ducklings soon learned how to take food; after I had been throwing it to them for a few minutes, they came and took it from my fingers. The mother was determined to fend off other ducks, attacking the larger mallards with impunity. As I fed the tufties, a young starling perched on the low rail by the water and began grabbing bread from my hand. Nearby a coot sat on its nest under a weeping willow a few yards from the path and, further along, the bank was covered in a herd of 58 coot basking in the early morning sun. Great crested grebes, which have nested here since 1983, were out on the water, and a family of long-tailed tits flipped through the willow trees. This tit is another bird which has firmly established itself in the park, with several pairs recorded in recent years. Over by Duck Island a dabchick sat on its nest not far from the pelican rock, the regular trill from its mate producing an interesting contrast with the boom of Big Ben.

One of the finest walks in London, especially in winter, is through the Royal Parks from Westminster to Kensington. When you have had your fill of wildfowl in St James's, there is the comparative solitude of Green Park. In January crows are already building their nests high in a plane tree by Clarence House, and the avenues of planes in Green Park look magnificent in the winter sun. During cold spells I have seen flocks of redwings and fieldfares foraging under the hawthorn trees by Piccadilly. Often, too, there are small flocks of mistle thrushes and chaffinches. Jays and magpies treat the park as a natural extension of Buckingham Palace gardens, which provides a sanctuary for birds in this part of London.

You can avoid the traffic at Hyde Park Corner by taking the subway through the tube station; for a moment you are back in the hustle and bustle of the city, but then the wide vista opens up of Hyde Park and the Serpentine. The little dell at the east end of the lake is always worth a visit. Its pools and waterfall attract birds at any season

*Common and black-headed gulls in the sanctuary on the Long Water – Kensington Gardens.* David Goode

and the fenced enclosure provides a tiny bird sanctuary in memory of W. H. Hudson, who was such a champion of wildlife in London's parks.

The Serpentine may have fewer wintering duck than St James's Park, but cormorants have taken to fishing here in recent years and there is quite a number of great crested grebes. Rarer birds sometimes appear, blown off course by gales or driven south by hard weather in northern Europe. Slavonian and red-necked grebes have both been reported in recent winters, and even a gannet and a razorbill. The lido is one of the most popular places for wildfowl and gulls to congregate; because it is fenced off from the public, the waterfowl can rest on the banks without being disturbed – until the occasional cold-weather-bathing addict comes on the scene.

Beyond the road bridge is the Long Water. The view from the bridge is one of remarkable tranquillity, contrasting with the constant passage of traffic on the road. Tree-clad banks extend to the ornamental fountains in the distance; pairs of grebes out on the water indulge in elaborate courtship rituals, and the odd heron fishes in the shallows. One autumn day I even watched a kingfisher diving for fish from the overhanging branches along the eastern bank. This part of the Serpentine has been set aside as a wildlife sanctuary since the 1920s. The path along its western side is worth an early morning visit. Rabbits of varying hue nibble the lakeside turf and surprisingly tame squirrels appear at your feet as soon as you produce a bag of food. Aylesbury and muscovy ducks add to the menagerie, and part-albino crows are always around, making the most of any scraps, but keeping their distance. Not far from the Peter Pan statue baskets of bird food hang from trees by the path; they are visited by an endless stream of tits, finches, sparrows and starlings. Great tits and blue tits will come on your hand to be fed at this particular spot.

The other bank of the Long Water by Peacock Walk is inaccessible and its dense growth of bramble provides an ideal nesting place for pochard and tufted duck. Recently, at the suggestion of the London Wildlife Trust, Parks staff installed an artificial bank of turves in the hope of encouraging kingfishers to nest. Special boxes for bats have been attached to the trees. Malcolm Kerr thinks that mandarin ducks would also nest here if suitable boxes were installed.

Continuing westwards, the walk brings you into the park landscape of Kensington Gardens, with its beautiful oaks and old stumps of sweet chestnut trees. This must be the nearest place to central London where you can see genuine woodland birds. Treecreepers and nuthatches nest in small numbers and even pied woodpeckers and tawny owls can sometimes be heard. Treecreepers are believed to have nested here since the 1920s. The nuthatch is a more recent addition; after nearly a century's absence from central parts of the city, it has benefited from London's cleaner atmosphere since the 1960s. Sadly, other birds have gone. A small colony of jackdaws survived until the 1950s, nesting in trees in the south-west corner of Kensington Gardens, but conditions apparently became less hospitable to them and they gradually died out; it seems unlikely that jackdaws will recolonise central London unless special efforts are made to encourage them. In contrast, there are now plenty of jays in Kensington Gardens, some of which are very tame. In autumn you can watch them stripping acorns from twigs a few feet above your head; this behaviour differs greatly from that of woodland jays, which sound their warning and flash into cover at the slightest sign of man.

The walk can be extended by crossing Kensington Church Street and going by way of Observatory Gardens to Holland Park: here is a wood of nearly 30 acres in the middle of Kensington. Holland Park was opened to the public when acquired by the London County Council in 1952. Before then it had been a private estate of the Holland family since the early seventeenth century. Most of the Jacobean mansion has long since gone, but the arcades and Orangery survive, and parts of the formal garden can still be seen. The original layout of the estate included formal gardens, lawns, and woodlands known as the 'Wildernesse'; remnants of the latter form the woods we see today.

Attractive woodland walks lead among the oaks and horse chestnuts, bordered by simple rustic fences to prevent disturbance of the wood on either side. These woods are full of undergrowth, with thick coverings of ivy on tree stumps and a tangle of bushes and shrubs; the scenery is quite unlike the open vistas of more formal parks. Garden and woodland birds abound, including plenty of robins, wrens, dunnocks and song thrushes, with occasional pairs of flycatchers, blackcaps, long-tailed tits and nuthatch. This is one of the few places in central London where the high-pitched song of goldcrests may be heard. Tawny owls have long been known to nest here; studies in the early seventies showed that in this urban situation they feed predominantly on birds, especially sparrows, feral pigeons, thrushes and starlings, whereas they would normally feed on voles and other small mammals. Interestingly, pellets from tawny owls collected in Hyde Park, Kensington Gardens and Regent's Park at the same time contained mainly the feathers of house sparrows, but remains of a wood mouse and noctule bat were also found.

Holland Park has other oddities – in particular, a collection of exotic birds, including crested cranes, ostriches and peacocks, whose cries bring an unreal quality to the wood, which is accentuated by free-range chickens pecking about under the trees and wild white rabbits scampering along the paths.

Each park has its own speciality. At Regent's Park it is the herons. Who would think that herons can be seen on their nests only ten minutes' walk from Madame Tussaud's? Three years ago 9 pairs raised 24 young in their treetop nests of the park's island heronry. Some of these herons fish on the Serpentine; others go to the lake in Battersea Park. I have even seen a heron dropping in to fish in Buckingham Palace gardens.

At Battersea the speciality nowadays must be the Canada geese. In late June 1985 there were nearly 300 on the lake, many of them newly hatched goslings. One morning all these geese were seen roosting in little huddles on the tables outside the cafeteria. They are not very popular with the park managers!

Over a period of 50 years Max Nicholson, a local resident and well-known ornithologist, has witnessed a dramatic change in the bird population of Battersea Park – from a 'sparrow-dominated regime' to a much greater variety. During his visits in April 1938, house sparrows and woodpigeons were by far the commonest birds. He described the park as infested with sparrows. Blackbirds, song thrushes and blue tits were reasonably common, but at that time robins, dunnocks, chaffinches and great tits were very scarce. No crows, jays or wrens were seen. By 1945 woodpigeons had virtually disappeared, as a result of organised shoots throughout the London area, but robins, wrens and greenfinches had colonised the park. They were all well established by 1950, when jays first appeared. Since then all the common garden birds have increased considerably. Crows, too, have taken up residence and jays have increased from the odd pair in 1950 to half a dozen pairs today. Magpies have also started nesting in the past few years. While the number of chaffinches nesting has declined in postwar years, that of greenfinches has grown dramatically, a feature seen elsewhere in central London. The most striking changes among the waterbirds are the recent breeding of great crested grebes and dabchicks, the massive build-up of Canada geese since the mid-seventies (which now probably outnumber the house sparrows) and an overall increase in winter wildfowl.

Battersea Park has a rather special wild patch. A secluded corner of the park, once used as an ash dump for the miniature railway, has been left to itself for many years and has developed a fascinating flora and fauna. It now forms an open grassy glade backed by tall trees of hornbeam, ash and elm, and surrounded on the other side by a bed of giant hogweed. The open glade is covered in yellow melilot and toadflax, pink-flowered mallow and self-heal. Cut-leaved cranesbill and enchanter's nightshade grow around the woodland edge and there are patches of hedge woundwort and lemon-scented balm. In an area little over an acre, bushes and trees provide nesting cover for 18 different species of bird, including blackcap and willow warbler. More surprising is the list of 17 different butterflies known to breed here, including speckled wood, common blue, purple hairstreak and even the white letter hairstreak, a most unusual occurrence in central London. While some of the butterflies are dependent on the flowers of the open glade, some of the rarer species are associated with the longer established trees. This tiny patch has now been set aside as a nature reserve. It owes its protection to Brian Mist, a local naturalist who has recorded the wildlife of the area for many years and has been a strong advocate of its protection. He is now officially a warden of the place, which has become known as Mist's Pitch.

In *Birds in London*, published in 1898, W. H. Hudson advocated that certain parts of the parks should be set aside as bird sanctuaries. Apparently it was his ideas which led to a special committee being set up over twenty years later to advise the Office of Works on appropriate sites in the Royal Parks. The committee suggested sanctuaries in Hyde Park, Kensington Gardens and Richmond Park. After the war, a further committee was appointed to continue this work, and for many years official observers kept records of the birds in each park. The series of reports published annually by the Ministry of Works in postwar years called *Birds in London* makes fascinating reading.

*This ornamental pond in Regent's Park provides a valuable sanctuary for waterbirds, including the nesting coot.*

*Greenwich Park, one of the royal parks, which contains a variety of birdlife including woodland birds in the mature parkland trees.*

Many of the suggestions made for improving parks as habitats for birds hold good today. Concern about shrubberies being 'trimmed to transparency', voiced by the committee in 1948, is a problem which is still very familiar. The committee also produced a comprehensive list for future plantings of appropriate trees and shrubs of value to birds, and advocated that reeds, sedges and yellow flag be planted in suitable places in ponds and lakes. At that time the emphasis was on making the most of conditions which already existed; little was said about creating entirely new habitats specifically for wildlife.

Now there is a strong move to create more natural habitats in parks. Belts of broad-leaved woodland of oak, ash, birch and other native trees have been planted in Battersea Park and at the new Mile End Park in the East End. In parts of Finsbury Park expanses of close-mown grass are being turned to hay meadows. Butterfly gardens composed of a variety of shrubs attractive to different butterflies have been planted; a fine example of this can be seen in the old kitchen garden at Kenwood House. New ponds are being dug to cater for the needs of wildlife rather than park lakes for boating and fishing. A small pond was recently dug in the nature reserve at Alexandra Park, and the pond in Waterlow Park at Highgate has been re-landscaped to cater for a greater variety of wildlife. These are just a few examples of a recent surge of activity to improve parks for wildlife.

The largest and wildest of London's parks is, of course, Richmond Park; two miles across and covering 2500 acres, it is by far the largest open space in London. Its wild vistas of heaths and woods are without parallel in the capital; nowhere else is there such a sense of untamed wilderness – even though it has in fact been shaped by man for centuries.

Before it was enclosed as a royal hunting park by Charles I in 1637, parts of Richmond Park were already farmland which had been 'reclaimed' from the pre-existing heath. This was particularly so in the eastern half of the park. Much of the western half was still open common land attached to Richmond, Petersham and Ham. Not surprisingly, enclosure of the park provoked much opposition from owners and commoners alike.

For 350 years Richmond has been a royal deer park, under the control of successive rangers appointed by the Crown (until 1910, when it was taken over by the Commissioners of Works). The park has changed considerably over that long period. Extensive tracts were once more thickly wooded with oak, which was cleared and transformed to open heath in the eighteenth century. Early last century new stands of oak were planted, and at that time there were considerable numbers of sheep and cows to be found.

The present landscape is a fine expanse of open park with clumps of woodland set amid acres of rough heath. Bracken and purple moor grass cover much of the open ground, with patches of rushes in the wetter parts. Poor acid soils on gravel support a variety of heathland plants; yellow tormentil and blue harebell may be seen among the coarse grasses, sedges and mosses.

For me the attraction of this particular variety of plants lies in their clear association with wild and wet. It comes as no surprise to flush snipe from among the rushes or hear a meadow pipit's spring song, for this has always been the sort of territory favoured by such birds. One afternoon in March a green woodpecker was out in the middle of the heath probing for insects among the tussocks of moor grass. As I walked towards the Pen Ponds, a pair of partridge broke cover and flew off noisily; by the pond, unusually tame reed buntings flitted around the feet of ducks and geese picking at crumbs as the waterfowl were fed.

Not far away a group of fallow deer lay contentedly in the winter sunshine, adding authenticity to the sense of wilderness. When Richmond was first enclosed, there were 1500 fallow deer and 200 red deer in the park. Their numbers have fluctuated over the years but gradually the herd of fallow deer has dwindled. Now the park supports some

600 deer of which more than half are fallow, the bucks being easily recognisable from their wide flat antlers. Until early this century the deer were kept in pens during the winter and fed on hay. Nowadays they are left to fend for themselves all year.

Richmond Park is probably best known for its deer. Groups grazing by the roadside, or just lying lazily beneath the trees on a summer's day, are a familiar sight. But it is a different matter in autumn when the rut is under way. Throaty roars of red deer stags carry far across the park as each gathers a group of hinds, and defends his herd against all comers. This is a time of open conflict between the stags, an annual ritual of the forest still observed.

Modern technology has brought a new look to Richmond Park in the past few years. To improve the quality of grass for the deer, sewage sludge has been spread over large areas. Used as a fertilizer, it counteracts the naturally poor soils, creating swathes of green luxuriance. No doubt the sludge gives better feeding for the deer, but I fear that this will only be at the expense of a host of other species, of animals and plants, which will inevitably disappear as their natural habitat is transformed. Fortunately the park is to be scheduled by the Nature Conservancy Council as a Site of Special Scientific Interest. This means that in future such fertilisation will most likely be prohibited because of the potential damage to wildlife.

---

*Fallow deer in Richmond Park.*

The ancient oaks of Richmond Park are one of its finest features. Some clearly date from before the time of enclosure. A row of massive oaks not far from Bog Lodge mark the boundary of a field which existed before Charles I had his grand idea. Oaks of this age are host to an extraordinary array of insects, as well as providing nesting holes for jackdaws, kestrels and tawny owls, or places for bats to breed and roost. An ancient oak can be a virtual nature reserve in itself, and Richmond Park has extensive groves of oaks whose value to wildlife is now appreciated. Some of the woods are set aside as sanctuaries. In others you can walk beneath the trees and hear noisy parties of jackdaws bringing their own brand of wild exuberance to the park, and the ringing laugh of a green woodpecker echoing through woodland which may have been growing for 500 years.

# ◆ CITY SQUARES ◆

THE INNUMERABLE leafy squares and formal gardens of central London have long been the envy of other capital cities. Mayfair, Bloomsbury and Belgravia were fashionable suburbs developed on an ambitious scale, with squares and gardens often forming their centrepieces. Such a focal point was Grosvenor Square; although the surrounding buildings have been almost entirely replaced since the war, and little of the original design survives, its six acres of land remain intact as the centre of the Grosvenor Estate, which was built in the 1730s. An engraving of 1754 shows the square devoid of any trees, with an ornately fenced formal garden occupying its central section. Belgravia was built a hundred years later, when Thomas Cubitt drained 140 acres of low-lying swampy fields south of Hyde Park Corner. By 1830 a fashionable district of Regency houses, including Belgrave Square and Eaton Square, stood where the marsh had been.

But not all London's squares were part of such a grand design. Throughout the city centre there is a multitude of more modest squares and gardens, each with its individual history. Some small, secluded town gardens of today, such as those attached to St Paul's at Covent Garden and St Giles in the Fields, were once country churchyards, when the churches literally stood in the fields. There are long-established gardens too, like the Inner Temple and the Abbey Garden at Westminster. Others, such as Lincoln's Inn Fields and Finsbury Circus by Liverpool Street, are remnants of the once extensive common lands around the city.

I suspect that some of the larger squares are now a good deal wilder than their designers originally intended. Most are now furnished with trees, rather than elegant ironwork, creating a kind of 'city woodland' that is a habitat all of its own. I remember flying over the West End some years ago en route to Heathrow and appreciating for the first time the vast acreage of trees in this part of London. Seen from above, their canopies formed a billowing sea of green among the well-ordered streets and rooftops of Belgravia and Kensington. Most are London planes, a tree which has been planted copiously throughout the capital over the past 200 years. It seems that this particular variety of plane arose as a hybrid between the oriental plane, first introduced in the sixteenth century and the western plane, which was brought back from Virginia in 1640 by the younger Tradescant. Some of the oldest examples are those planted in 1789 in Berkeley Square; and in Carshalton there is a magnificent plane which is claimed to be the tallest tree in London.

*Plane tree by the House of Lords.*

The popularity of the London plane as a street tree was largely due to its remarkable ability to withstand the grimy atmosphere of the capital. Even in 1700, the city was suffering greatly from the effects of burning coal, and by 1730 it was well established that certain trees could no longer be grown there. But the plane was able to tolerate the smoke and sooty deposits – perhaps because of its habit of periodically shedding the outer layers of bark. It is a most attractive tree, especially in winter, when its golden fruits are pendulous in the winter sun and its brindled, brown and yellow bark can be seen at its best.

But the plane does have disadvantages. Because it is in an alien environment, unlike our native trees it is not endowed with a rich assortment of insect life. Some insects, such as the vapourer moth, with its grotesque tufted caterpillars, do use it as a food source. But, apart from these and a few others, there is little to attract warblers or other insect-eating birds to these relatively lifeless canopies.

So, as habitats for wildlife, these exotic city trees are somewhat disappointing. They do, of course, provide places for certain birds to nest and roost, but the variety of birds in the central squares and gardens depends essentially on how these open spaces are used. Whether they are given over entirely to close-mown grass or whether there are flowerbeds and shrubberies makes all the difference. The number of people using the square is important too. In those squares consisting largely of mown grass and a fringe of plane trees you will be lucky to see more than half a dozen different sorts of birds. Feral pigeons and house sparrows will be there for certain; they are used to being fed. There may also be the odd pair of woodpigeons. Black-headed gulls frequent many of the larger squares and gardens; they are quite a sight in the Embankment gardens at Westminster, where they line up along the wall next to each of the seats, waiting to be fed. Starlings are ubiquitous where there is food to be had. If the square is big enough, with sufficient grass, you might spot a pair of blackbirds; and a few acres of grass are needed to attract a pair of mistle thrushes. There might be a crow's nest in the top of a plane tree. And that's about it.

But it is a different matter if there are flowerbeds and shrubberies. Exposed soil is a scarce commodity in central London, so even a small patch can be vital to a pair of grubbing blackbirds. Shrubberies have an even greater influence. An overgrown shrubbery is about the nearest point to wildness that any of these squares or gardens is allowed to reach. For the birds it is far more than a group of ornamental plants. The berries are important as food; but the thicket of bushes is probably more significant – it provides a habitat where there is plenty of cover, where spiders spin their webs, and robins and dunnocks search among the fallen leaves for anything that moves. The shrubbery is also a place where few people go, a corner of the square which forms a real sanctuary for birds.

Take Belgrave Square for example. It consists of about five acres; a very busy road encircles the gardens, which are open only to residents of the square. Within the fence is a peripheral belt of mature trees and extensive shrubberies, while the central part is an open area of grass with a tennis court. From 1978 to 1980 Leo Batten, who worked in the nearby office of the Nature Conservancy Council, kept a record of all the birds

Opposite *Pendant fruits of plane trees along the embankment.*

which bred within these gardens. He found that, over the three years, there was an average of 33 pairs of birds of 14 different species. Looking through the traffic to these gardens, it hardly seems possible that they could harbour such a variety. Blackbirds were most numerous, with up to 9 pairs in one year – it is an ideal habitat for them, with a good mixture of shrubberies and open glades. Next most abundant, with about 6 pairs, was the dunnock. This is a familiar bird in suburban gardens, perhaps one of the commonest breeding birds in the whole of London, but would not normally be expected in such numbers in central London – it probably benefits from the secluded nature of the gardens. Trees in the square generally held about five nests of the woodpigeon or ringdove. Early in the year there was always one occupied crow's nest in the top of a tree. At least one pair of song thrushes bred every year, and once there was also a pair of mistle thrushes. Two or 3 pairs of greenfinches nested – their attractive song flight could be heard around the square each spring, the cock bird frequently using the huge wireless aerials on a nearby embassy roof as a songpost. A few robins were always present, and up to 3 pairs nested. Similarly, there were 2 or 3 pairs of bluetits and 1 pair of great tits. No wrens nested for two years, but then there were 2 pairs the following year. A few feral pigeons bred most years. Perhaps the most notable birds were a pair of goldfinches which nested in 1979 and the single pair of spotted flycatchers that nested every year.

*In many of London's squares, including Bedford Square, the mixture of habitats attracts a variety of birdlife such as blackbirds, greenfinch, carrion crows and great tits.* David Goode

Opposite *Back gardens in Brockley; a valuable habitat for wildlife. Winter visitors include redwings and siskins.*

Belgrave Square is perhaps not quite wild enough for blackcaps or other warblers. But many of the birds now breeding there were rarely known to nest in central London 30 years ago. The goldfinch first started to nest in places like Battersea Park and Brompton Cemetery in the early 1950s, and at that time greenfinches too were predominantly suburban birds with only 1 or 2 pairs in the central parks. Even the blackbird is a relative newcomer to city-centre life. It was first known to nest in Bloomsbury in 1935 and, by 1937, nested in Lincoln's Inn Fields. Though it gradually spread into other central areas, it was still by no means common in the 1950s. Now blackbirds have moved into all kinds of central locations. In 1984 a pair built their nest behind the ornate masonry crest by the St Stephen's entrance to the Houses of Parliament. Later this pair were feeding their newly fledged young on the grass around St Margaret's Church in Parliament Square. In 1985 a pair nested by an entrance to County Hall on a stone ledge overhung by a bush of prostrate cotoneaster. Another nested in a narrow street by Covent Garden where they were often seen hopefully digging for worms in windowboxes; despite the absence of greenery, they managed to rear their brood successfully.

Many central London squares now have a fair share of the commoner birds, and an early morning visit in May may be rewarded by a respectable dawn chorus. Even some of the less likely squares can be of interest. Not far from Liverpool Street station is Finsbury Circus, the largest open space in the City. Here, in a small garden with a bowling green set among plane trees, 2 cock blackbirds were singing their hearts out early one Good Friday morning. Their voices reverberated around the buildings of the circus in the strangely quiet City streets. Above, a pair of greenfinches were calling, the cock bird performing his delightful song-flight around the tops of the plane trees. A pair of woodpigeons were busy constructing their flat platform of a nest on an overhanging branch forty feet above the street. From the bowling green came the 'chissick' call of a pied wagtail, and a party of 4 carrion crows honked noisily over the rooftops. Gone is the time only 30 years ago when crows avoided nesting in the public squares. Now there are treetop nests in virtually every sizeable square in central London. Even the close confines of St James's Square off Pall Mall has crows nests, where the comings and goings of the birds can be watched from surrounding buildings.

In recent years house martins have made a comeback in central London and are now nesting in Knightsbridge and Belgrave Square. This was unheard of ten years ago, but by 1982 there were 120 pairs nesting on buildings in inner London. One particular colony on the French Embassy at Albert Gate has gone from strength to strength. These birds have developed the curious habit of building their nests within the ornate 'roses' in the stonework beneath the eaves. In 1985 large numbers of martins were feeding over St James's Park; they constantly made sorties over Horseguards Parade to examine the eaves of the Foreign Office, as if to see if it would be suitable for next year's nest.

Mallard ducks have long been known to breed in close proximity with man and some have become quite accustomed to city life. In the early 1930s a pair nested for two successive years at the pond in New Square by Lincoln's Inn. But they do not always nest by water. In recent years there have been many instances of ducks nesting in secluded corners of city squares and gardens. In the spring of 1982 a pair even nested in the enclosed courtyard of an office building in Essex Road not far from Islington Green, where the nearest water was a quarter of a mile away at the Regents Canal. One pair regularly nests at the Guildhall, and when the chicks hatch a police escort is needed to see the brood across busy London Wall to the nearest pond in the Barbican. Others even nest in window boxes at the Barbican from which the newly fledged ducklings have to fall 40 feet to the pavement. Somehow they manage to survive. Another has its nest in a shrubbery below Big Ben at Westminster. From here the duck leads its brood across Parliament Square and into St James's Park. It proceeds in a determined manner, oblivious to the traffic, which is brought to a halt. I am told that even the Prime Minister was kept waiting on one occasion while the ducklings safely crossed the road by the entrance to the House of Commons.

There is quite a lot of plant life to be found even around the streets and the buildings of central London. Ten years ago a detailed record was kept by a local botanist, Rosalind Hadden, of all the plants growing wild within the postal district of W1. The area surveyed covered all the streets north of Piccadilly as far as Marylebone Road. Mayfair, Soho and Marylebone are all included and, apart from the large squares such as Berkeley, Grosvenor and Portman, there are no extensive areas of green. Yet within this area a total of 157 plants were recorded. They were not, on the whole, found in the gardens of the town squares where you might expect them to be, but were growing in all kinds of surprising places.

Sixty-one different plants were growing on the stonework of pavements, walls and buildings. These included such oddities as knotted hedge parsley in the masonry of St Mary's Church in Bryanston Square, garden parsley sprouting from a wall in Montague Street, and hairy finger grass from a crack in the pavement in Upper Montague Street. Ferns on the stonework included bracken, hart's-tongue fern, broad buckler fern, male fern and lady fern. There was even an introduced relative of the bracken called ribbon fern. Saplings of shrubs and trees included tree of heaven, sycamore, elm, goat willows, buddleia and even a birch sapling about three feet high growing out of a bare wall near Madame Tussaud's.

Nearly 100 different kinds of plants were noted in patches of soil such as window boxes, paths, flowerbeds and lawns. Some were quite unexpected and had little chance of survival, such as the blinks and lesser spearwort, both water-loving plants, found in a flowerbed at Paddington Street Gardens. Perhaps they had been introduced with a load of peat. Another oddity was burnet saxifrage in a lawn near Park Crescent. Perhaps the strangest sight was a sapling of ash about ten feet high growing out of a six-inch window box.

◆ THREE ◆

# LOSSES AND GAINS

# ◆LOSSES◆

LOOKING AT LONDON today it is difficult to visualise a time when there were beavers in the rivers and multitudes of red kites scavenging in the streets. But the name of Beverley Brook in Richmond is a reminder that beavers once occurred, even though it was over 1000 years ago and they have been extinct in Britain for the past 600 years. We have more direct knowledge of kites from descriptions during the fifteenth century, when they were said to be so tame that children fed them on bread. At that time both kites and ravens were protected because they were useful for cleaning up the rubbish in the streets. Kites were last known to nest in London at Gray's Inn in 1777 and ravens persisted for about another 50 years. Nowadays red kites are found only in the hills of mid-Wales, and the nearest wild ravens to London nest on the sea cliffs of Dorset and the Isle of Wight. Similarly, polecats and pine martens, now rare animals of the western uplands, were occasionally seen in places like Epping Forest only a century ago. Other species have disappeared more recently. In 1945, Fitter wrote, 'Otters are commoner than most people think.' They could still be seen from time to time in the Lea Valley. Now otters have gone completely from the London area, as they have from so much of lowland England. Hares too have declined in the past twenty years and you will be lucky to see one now in Greater London.

There are many reasons for these losses; each species has been affected in different ways. Kites and ravens disappeared as sanitation improved and they were no longer protected. Polecats and pine martens were exterminated by gamekeepers, and otters have suffered a prolonged decline as a result of hunting, river 'improvements' and disturbance of their habitats. Several birds which were common in the countryside around London 80 years ago have suffered a similar national decline. The red-backed shrike, nightjar and wryneck are perhaps the most striking examples. Each species has rather special requirements and their decline may well have resulted from a progressive reduction in suitable habitats; though it has been suggested that slight shifts in weather conditions could also have had an effect. These are birds that like warm dry summers.

A clear picture of the natural history of London a hundred years ago can be gained from the writings of Richard Jefferies and W. H. Hudson, both of whom described the everyday wildlife to which they were accustomed. In his account of a train journey to Brighton in about 1880, Jefferies mentions that:

> butcher birds or shrikes are frequently found on the telegraph wires. From that elevation they pounce down on their prey and return to the wire. There were two pairs of shrikes using the telegraph wires for this purpose one spring only a short distance beyond noisy Clapham Junction.

In the early years of this century Jefferies found the shrike to be a common summer visitor to the hedges and thickets around London, in places which are now within the outer suburbs. But there has since been a dramatic decline, and by 1964 only 20 pairs were thought to nest within 20 miles of St Paul's. That year was the last in which I saw shrikes in the area, and even that sighting was at Leith Hill, well beyond the limits of the city. Sadly they are no longer to be found breeding anywhere near London and have become very scarce elsewhere in southern England. If Richard Jefferies were able to tramp his fields and footpaths again, I am sure this would be one bird which he would sorely miss.

It is certainly a very long time since a nightingale sang in Berkeley Square – if it ever did! But now the bird is on the verge of disappearing entirely from London. Richard Jefferies obviously loved to hear the nightingales at Surbiton, where he lived between 1877 and 1882. One of his favourite places was a copse where 4 or 5 nightingales sang in the spring, and he even heard one singing across the road from his house. In one of his essays in *Nature Near London*, he described a little orchard by the side of a road where 'a nightingale sang under the shadow of a hornbeam for hours every morning while the "City" men were hurrying past to their train'.

The nightingale was also well known to W. H. Hudson in the 1890s. It was apparently common in the grounds of Christ's Hospital by Bostall Woods but, more surprisingly, he also heard it at Streatham Common, where it nested only six and a half miles from Charing Cross. Charles Dixon's account of birdlife in London suggests that the nightingale was still very abundant in the early years of this century:

> The vast Metropolitan area is exceptionally well favoured by the nightingale. Indeed it is only the lack of suitable conditions, such as proper cover and food, that arrests its distribution short of the most central parts of London.

But Dixon was aware that it had already gone from some of its former haunts, such as Harrow Road near Kensal Rise, where, it is said, Dickens and Thackeray used to walk to hear the nightingales. Although it was decreasing in some parts of Middlesex, the bird could still be heard all around the fringes of London, especially at Balham, Tooting, Clapham, Norwood and Wimbledon in south London, and at Osterley Park and in Epping Forest to the north. But by the 1940s Fitter noted that it had declined considerably. By then, the nearest breeding place to central London was Ham Common near Richmond, though 'further out at Bookham and Epping the nightingale still abounds'.

The nightingale's decline has continued. Now there are few spots in London where you can be sure of hearing its song. One is Hainault Forest. In 1985 several were singing there on 18 April, a regular date for their arrival in the spring. There are other localities around Biggin Hill where it may be heard, but in this southern fringe of London you really have to travel into the countryside of Surrey or Kent to be sure of finding a nightingale.

Part of the reason for the nightingale's decline in London is the reduction of suitable habitat. The bird prefers thickets of scrub rather than woodland. But this is not the whole answer: there are places which appear suitable which have nevertheless lost their nightingales.

The enormous spread of London over the past century has lead to the destruction of huge areas of natural habitat, and many specialised plants and animals have suffered as a result. Grasshopper warblers and wood warblers, for example, and plants such as lily of the valley, solomon's seal, butcher's broom, bog heather and sundew have become restricted to a few suitable localities. The original variety of wildlife is found only in places where the natural habitats survive intact.

Increasing urban pressures have also taken their toll. During the first half of this century it was common practice for people to pick woodland and meadow flowers wherever they were easily accessible. As a result, primroses and cowslips virtually disappeared from many parts of London. During the same period the level of air pollution was such that many sensitive species of plants and insects were unable to exist in central areas.

One bird which has suffered directly from the expansion of London is the rook. Rooks are usually associated with open farmland, and their treetop rookeries are a familiar feature of towns and villages through the length and breadth of Britain. But there was a time when London boasted its own rookeries, some in the very centre of the city. One of the most famous was in the trees of the Inner Temple, near Fleet Street, where there was a thriving colony until about 1830. A few birds continued to build nests there as late as 1916. In the early days of this century there was a flourishing rookery at Gray's Inn, and the birds were still nesting at Connaught Square, only a hundred yards from Marble Arch. But by that time most of the inner London rookeries were gradually dying out. The Kensington Gardens colony started to decline in about 1880, and another colony at Clapham Common was deserted by 1905.

Rooks are dependent on farmland for their food. As London spread, engulfing more and more farmland, so the rooks nesting in central London had to make longer and longer journeys to feed. Charles Dixon, writing about the birds' plight in 1909, put it very well when he said:

> The earliest settlers in some of these London rookeries found their food in the fields below the trees; their latest descendants have to fly miles to and fro for every morsel they eat or on which they nourish their broods.

Unlike many Londoners, who moved out to live in the new suburbs as the city expanded, the rooks at first maintained allegiance to their traditional home. For many years they remained remarkably faithful to particular rookeries, but the ever-increasing distance to their feeding grounds gradually took its toll. One by one the central London rookeries fell silent. Now you have to go out to farmland on the borders of Essex, Kent or Hertfordshire to see a rookery.

◆

# ◆GAINS◆

THE FLORA AND FAUNA of London is continually changing, but not all the changes have been for the worse. In fact, it could be argued that the gains more than compensate for the losses. Many species have increased substantially, and there has also been a large number of total newcomers. The reasons for this are varied. Some animals have benefited from a lack of persecution – the fox and carrion crow, for example, and maybe the kestrel too. Some species have increased dramatically during the past 10 or 20 years as a result of cleaner air and water. House martins are breeding again in central London, and the growing number of waterfowl on the Thames is a clear sign of better conditions. New habitats such as reservoirs and gravel pits have also contributed to the greater number and variety of waterfowl (see pages 72–92).

A few species of birds are newcomers to London because they have spread from other areas. Collared doves, black redstarts and little ringed plovers have all colonised the capital during this century. Other species, such as the huge flocks of winter gulls, have become well adapted to an urban lifestyle. Yet others have been introduced, either intentionally or quite by chance, and have managed to survive the rigours of the city.

*Feral pigeons, descendants of the cliff-nesting rock dove, find London's buildings make a natural home.*
David Goode

*Since being introduced to London in 1905 the grey squirrel has been enormously successful. It is now commonly seen throughout the capital in woods, parks and gardens.* David Goode

Some have thrived to such an extent that they have come to be regarded as pests – the grey squirrel, for example, which, despite its appealing behaviour, is far from popular with park keepers because of the damage it causes to trees. Even the recently arrived Canada geese are posing problems for park managers in some places and need to be controlled.

These reservations apart, the following pages examine in more detail those species of birds and animals whose increase has contributed so much to enriching the city's environment.

## ◆ *Crows, jays and magpies* ◆

Among the many birds which have increased dramatically in London in recent times, three deserve special mention: the carrion crow, jay and magpie. If you walk around the central London parks, you are certain to see all three of them sooner or later. Carrion crows, with their treetop nests dotted around the parks and city squares, seem to be everywhere. Jays and magpies can regularly be seen in Kensington Gardens and Holland Park, and magpies nest even in St James's Park. Out in the suburbs all three are fairly common, especially where there are parks or large gardens with plenty of trees.

This has not always been the case. As members of the crow family, these birds were heavily persecuted last century because of the damage they did to nesting gamebirds, and by 1900 all of them were very scarce indeed. They have certainly benefited from the changing attitudes towards such birds in towns, for no longer are they automatically regarded as vermin and shot on sight. When he wrote about the birdlife of London in 1909, Charles Dixon advocated protection of the jay; he regarded it as a gradually declining species which at that time was totally absent from central London. He suggested that:

> [it] should be protected and encouraged in all parts of London; indeed efforts should be made to introduce this beautiful species into the large parks which contain suitable cover. There is nothing to prevent it from becoming a denizen of these, where its handsome plumage would prove an additional charm.

The crow was the first of the three to increase. From its footholds in the outer London suburbs, where it had never been totally eradicated, the crow started to spread back towards the centre. It was noticeably more abundant in the 1930s, and after the Second World War its numbers suddenly grew enormously. By 1950 it was breeding throughout London; it was still scarce in the heavily built-up central areas, but was nesting in many of the parks and even in some of the more secluded inner London squares.

Over the past 30 years crows have become very common indeed. Far from being wary birds which fly off at the first sight of man, they are now a familiar part of the urban scene. Their massive bills and iridescent black plumage make them highly distinctive. Some of those in the central parks are partly albino with varying amounts of white, especially in the wings. Every day at low tide crows can be seen poking around on the exposed mud and shingle banks of the Thames in central London. Some have taken to scavenging as a way of life, and in the winter months hundreds congregate at refuse tips where they vie with the gulls for scraps of food. Others feed in parks and on playing fields, where they probe for insects in the turf. In Hyde Park some of the crows are remarkably tame; they will hop around on the grass within a yard or two of you, making sideways jumps to pick up morsels of food – but they are away as soon as a dog comes near.

Last year a pair of crows nested in a plane tree on the Victoria Embankment at the foot of Northumberland Avenue. They are early nesters, sitting on eggs during cold February winds. By April they had young in the nest and there was a constant coming and going for deliveries of food. It was possible to watch these birds feeding their young from the platform of Charing Cross station. By the first week of May, long before the leaves were on the tree, the young had flown.

Outside the breeding season crows roost colonially, and one of the most spectacular wildlife sights in London is the pre-roost gathering at dusk on Wimbledon Common or Hampstead Heath. I do not know who suggested that crows are solitary birds; evidently they had never experienced one of these roosts. The birds arrive in ones or twos, or even in small parties, during the late afternoon, and as dusk falls there is a huge gathering. By mid-December there are often over 1000 birds in the roost at Wimbledon, and at Ken Wood there may be 500 or 600. Other roosts are scattered around London, including one on a small island in the Thames at Chiswick and another on trees at Walthamstow Reservoir.

The jay has not become quite such a metropolitan bird as the crow; it still prefers places with plenty of trees. But, since recolonising the parks in the 1930s, it is now found throughout much of London, and is even familiar as a garden bird. Richard Jefferies's contention that 'If not so constantly shot at the jay would be anything but wild' has been proved correct. Like the crows, some of the jays in the parks are surprisingly tame. In the autumn you can watch them stripping acorns from the oaks in Kensington Gardens while you stand beneath the trees. They are equally tame in Holland Park, where they will even come for food. Especially in the outer suburbs, jays have become well adapted to domestic gardens. They readily come to bird tables for food, and many people actively encourage them to do so, even though they are known to rob the nests of other garden birds. I must admit that I enjoy watching the antics of jays in the garden and always ensure that they have a good supply of monkey nuts in the winter.

*A crow's nest in Victoria Embankment Gardens by the National Liberal Club.*

The magpie has taken much longer to spread through the capital, but it is rapidly catching up. In the late 1950s Stanley Cramp found that the bird was well established on Hampstead Heath and visiting the central area more frequently than it had done before. Writing in *Birds of the London Area* in 1964, he was hopeful that it would join its successful relatives as a breeding species in inner London. Since then, magpies seem to have proliferated and are now firmly established in the larger parks, even in the city centre. A pair has been in residence around the Lido in Hyde Park during the past two years. They have also nested in Battersea, Regent's and St James's Parks, and in Buckingham Palace Gardens. Although often regarded as a bird of open countryside, over the past 20 years the magpie has gradually been adapting to a more urban way of life. Its spread into London has been paralleled in other cities, and it has recently become much more familiar in suburban gardens. When today's blackbirds hatch their young, it seems that they are forever having to see off marauding magpies.

## ◆ *Ring-necked parakeets* ◆

Of all the recent additions to the birdlife of London, the ring-necked parakeet must rank as one of the most curious. No doubt it all started with the occasional birds escaping from aviaries, but they have adapted themselves remarkably well to London's environment. Now there are considerable numbers of these small green parrots living completely wild in the suburbs.

In its native haunts of subtropical Africa and Asia, this bird occurs in a great variety of habitats. It seems to be equally at home in the rhododendron-covered foothills of the Himalayas as in the plains of India, or in the arid regions of North Africa. In some parts of India it frequents towns and villages, where it appears to be well suited to living in close association with man, feeding around the houses on grain and fruit, and frequently perching on the rooftops.

As long ago as the early 1930s a few were living wild in gardens near Epping. Apparently they had escaped from a local aviary, but there is no evidence that they ever nested in the wild. Since then other sightings occurred from time to time, but it was not until the late 1960s that people suddenly became aware of wild parakeets in a number of London suburbs. In 1969 they were seen in several places between Croydon and Bromley. The first definite evidence of breeding came from Croydon in 1971 but, from the number of birds seen that year, it seems likely that they had already been nesting successfully for several years. In the same year there was a flock of up to 22 on the other side of London, around Woodford Green and Higham Park near Walthamstow. Over the next ten years numbers continued to grow and they gradually colonised new areas. By the winter of 1981, there were over 100 parakeets roosting regularly at Beckenham, and this was only one of several London roosts.

Nowadays their strongholds seem to be around Brentford in west London and in the southern suburbs from Carshalton to Sidcup. In these areas parakeets have developed an affinity for particular parks or woodlands, seemingly favouring places where there are plenty of old trees. One of the best places to observe them in west London is in the grounds of Chiswick House. In the tranquillity of this park it is extraordinary suddenly to see a noisy flock of bright green parrots flying through the trees and out over the cricket pitch. But the sight is not unusual, especially on a summer's evening. Early in the year, while nesting, they are relatively inconspicuous, but once they start to roost communally they are all too obvious. Those at Chiswick and the few pairs in Osterley Park generally nest in holes in trees. They are frequently seen in Kew Gardens too, where it somehow is less surprising to encounter such exotic birds.

Further up the Thames at Runnymede a flock has used an island in the river for many years as a winter roosting site. They are also known to nest at Shepperton Studios, not far away. During the winter, flocks are seen from time to time by birdwatchers at the nearby Wraysbury gravel pits. Two years ago a flock of 51 appeared there early in December, providing a startling contrast with the winter flocks of gulls and wildfowl. Parakeets seem able to survive even the hardest of winters, and in some parts of London they have become regular visitors to birdtables, especially if peanuts are available. Some have even been seen in the autumn feeding on sunflower heads.

In the southern suburbs parakeets have nested for a number of years at Park Langley and are also known to breed at Scadbury Park, Petts Wood, Foots Cray Meadow, and probably also at Beckenham Place Park. In recent years they have also been in residence at Greenwich Park and other places on the fringe of inner London. A regular winter roost of 50 or 60 birds has been established at Hither Green Cemetery not far from New Cross; it is startling to see the bright green flocks of birds flying in to roost over snow-covered tombstones.

For novelty, top marks must go to a pair of parakeets at Beddington Park near Croydon. In 1985 I was amused to see that they were nesting in a ginkgo tree. Passersby on the footpath beside the church were oblivious of the green parrots with bright red beaks perched on a branch above their heads. But, for me, the presence of these exotic birds in a tree of ancient lineage from the far side of the world was rather pleasing – and certainly the last thing I would have expected in suburban London.

## ◆ Kestrels ◆

Writing in the 1890s on the scarcity of the kestrel in the London area, W. H. Hudson said he thought it extremely improbable that the bird would ever return to the capital. He was mistaken. During the twentieth century it has gradually spread back into London from the outlying suburbs. Not only has it increased, but it has become thoroughly adapted to urban conditions. Now it can be found in virtually any part of London, including the heart of the city, where it is often to be seen hunting over the rooftops.

The history of the kestrel's return makes interesting reading. According to Dixon, it could be found in suitable localities around the edge of London during the early 1900s but was still decreasing in many areas. Although it was regularly seen in the central London parks, it was not breeding within a fifteen-mile radius of the centre. At that time the sparrowhawk was much commoner in the inner London suburbs and was often breeding in places where kestrels were entirely absent.

In 1928 a kestrel's nest was found on a chimney of the old LCC tramway power station at Greenwich, and in 1931 a pair nested on St Paul's School in Hammersmith. This was the first kestrel's nest known in the inner part of London for over 50 years.

The bird continued to spread, and by the 1940s a pair was nesting regularly on either Westminster Abbey or the tower above the House of Lords. In the immediate postwar years there was a sudden growth in numbers. Two pairs nested on bombed-out buildings in the City, and by 1950, 5 pairs had nests within an area comprising fewer than ten square miles of central London. By the late 1950s, kestrels were nesting throughout the capital, by which time they seemed to have become totally adjusted to urban and suburban life. According to a detailed survey between 1968 and 1972, kestrels were thought to be nesting in 377 different places within 20 miles of St Paul's Cathedral. There are now over 100 pairs nesting regularly within Greater London.

*Kestrels are often to be seen in central London where they nest in a variety of places including the window ledges of office blocks.* Alan Parker

The kestrel's comeback may have been due in part to reduced levels of persecution, as the result of the decline in gamekeeping over the past 40 years. At one time a keeper's gibbet would, as a matter of course, have included the remains of several kestrels, and it is likely that few young birds would have survived to colonise new areas. A more enlightened and tolerant attitude towards birds of prey now prevails. Instead of being shot on sight, they are now accepted, and some people even go to great lengths to encourage them. Last year the Thames Water Authority made special efforts to erect a nesting box for kestrels on its building near Walthamstow, when their previous nest site had been destroyed. Other people have successfully induced them to settle in central London by putting nest boxes on tall office blocks.

An element of adaptation has played a part in the way kestrels have colonised built-up areas. In the countryside, they normally feed on voles or insects. You only have to see them hovering by the side of motorways to realise that their prey is to be found in the rough grassland of the banks and verges. But in the city they have taken to catching small birds, especially house sparrows, and these now form a substantial part of their diet. (A more unusual diet consists of scraps of hamburger scavenged by kestrels at Forest Hill School after the lunch break!) From an office window in Belgravia I often watched a pair which had nested near Cadogan Square. Only very rarely would they hover above the buildings. Instead, they would drift along the rooftops on the lookout for unsuspecting sparrows. Flying alongside the adjacent mews, they might catch a bird unawares on a window ledge. This is a very different kind of hunting from hanging on the updraft above a downland scarp, but they seem to be successful at it.

On one occasion, again in Belgravia, I remember a commotion as a pigeon tried frantically to get away from a pursuing kestrel. Both birds landed on the ornate façade of a building opposite my window. The kestrel landed on a ledge a foot or two above the pigeon, which peered upwards nervously, unsure whether its pursuer was still there. After a moment the kestrel flew off, leaving me doubting if it would actually be capable of catching a healthy pigeon. More recently, a pair have been nesting somewhere in the vicinity of King's College on the Strand and I have several times seen them soaring overhead carrying food – usually something about the size of a sparrow.

Nowadays kestrels choose a wide variety of places for their nests. In parks and woodland they will use hollow trees, if suitable holes are available. Regularly in recent years a pair has nested in a hollow tree within yards of a footpath across Hampstead Heath. From one position you can see into the nest, and local people in the know will often stop to watch what they are doing. It is amazing that these birds manage to rear their young in so public a place, but they have been successful, and this might explain why several of the kestrels around the heath are remarkably tame. At Richmond Park, too, there is a great number of kestrels nesting in close proximity to one another in the ancient oaks, which are riddled with holes. In 1967, 20 pairs are recorded as having nested in the park.

Some kestrels use old crows' nests in trees, and one pair at Riddlesdown quarry near Purley use a hole high up on the chalk face alongside a noisy colony of jackdaws. But it is on buildings and other artificial structures that kestrels find some of the more unusual places to nest. Church towers and steeples are among the more popular venues. In recent years quite a few central London churches have played host to kestrels, including St Matthew's next to the Department of Environment offices in Marsham Street, St Dunstan's near the Tower of London, St Luke's off Sydney Street in Chelsea, and another St Luke's in Redcliffe Gardens near Earl's Court. Other central London buildings used as nesting sites include Bankside power station, the British Rail headquarters at Marylebone, Victoria station, Guy's Hospital, the Law Courts in the Strand and, most appropriately, the Natural History Museum.

One year a pair of kestrels nested on a gasometer at Old Oak Common, and for the past two years I have seen another in what may originally have been a crow's nest high on an electricity pylon at Hackney Marshes. In 1985 a pair delighted office workers in the City by nesting on the waterfront pub called the Samuel Pepys, where, early in July, the air was filled with the calls of their offspring.

### ◆ Gulls ◆

Every day throughout the winter, morning and evening, strings of gulls can be seen flying high over London. At Clapham Junction station late on a winter's afternoon there is a continuous stream of them; long straggling lines heading westwards into the sunset. Watch them for a few minutes from any good vantage point and you will soon realise that hundreds are passing over, along a flightline as regular as the aircraft heading for Heathrow. These are the commuters of the bird world. Day after day they follow the same route from roost to feeding grounds and back again. So regular are their daily journeys that they would certainly benefit from a six-month season ticket from October to March.

We used to call them seagulls but, apart from crossing the sea on their way to and from breeding grounds in northern Europe, these birds spend little of their time at sea. For the winter months they come to London, and while here their lifestyle is bound up completely with our own. Dependent on man for food and safe places to roost at night, they are exploiters of the city *par excellence*. Inadvertently we have given them precisely what they need to survive the winter. By night thousands roost on reservoirs at Staines and in the Lea Valley. Even at Barn Elms, close to Fulham, huge flocks of black-headed gulls gather every night. But, though offering ideal conditions for a drink and a wash, the reservoirs provide little in the way of food – which is why the gulls must journey back and forth each day.

Having learned to make the most of our wasteful feeding habits, the gulls thrive on what seven million people throw away each day: scraps of unwanted food by the ton are concentrated for them at municipal refuse tips. Here they find plentiful sustenance, with regular fresh deliveries. Even in the hardest frost they have little difficulty obtaining enough to eat. Flying up to sixty miles daily is well worth it.

Rubbish tips are not everyone's pleasure. The all-pervasive smell and the revolting fences of high netting full of wind-blown trash are enough to put anyone off. But behind those fences is an amazing scene as hundreds of black-headed gulls vie with each other for the best pickings. Oblivious of man, obsessed with food, they dash and pick and grab, often right in front of working bulldozers. The standard practice nowadays at these tips is for the refuse to be covered by soil, but if substantial areas are left uncovered then the larger gulls move in – they prefer to feed away from the mêlée around the bulldozers. Crows, too, are often to be seen among the gulls, poking about for scraps. At times the air is filled with raucous cries, especially when the larger gulls chase others to make them drop their food. But there is far more food available than the birds can possibly eat and much of their day is spent resting. Huge flocks gather in fields or on lakes around the rubbish tips. Sometimes they use the roofs of nearby buildings for their siesta. Then, in the afternoon, they set off back to the nightly roost.

With an office overlooking the river at Westminster, I am always conscious of the gulls' return from their northerly breeding grounds. Some lesser black-backed gulls reappear as early as June or July, when you might expect them to be busy raising young somewhere on the coast of Norway – maybe these are non-breeding birds. At first it is only single birds drifting along the river by Westminster Bridge, but these big gulls with their blue-black wings are very conspicuous after an absence of several months. They are a sure sign that migration is under way. Later in July there is a steady trickle of birds passing along the river all day long, apparently heading for the reservoirs near Heathrow. In 1983, about 500 had arrived by the end of June, and during the next month the flock built up to over 1000 birds. These early arrivals may not stay in the London area for long. They are probably on their way to winter in Spain or Portugal.

At this time, too, a few black-headed gulls start to arrive, but it is not until the autumn that large numbers of these smallest of our gulls return from the continent. During October and November, many thousands appear in London, where they will stay for the winter. They can be seen all along the strandline of the Thames and around park lakes, where they soon take to being fed. But it is at their nightly roosts that you will see the largest gatherings. In November 1983, local birdwatchers estimated that there were 27,000 flying in to roost at Barn Elms reservoir. The black-headed are by far the commonest of the winter gulls, but others also spend the winter here. Common gulls start to appear in September or October and, so long as the weather is mild, large flocks can be seen feeding on school playing fields and in open parkland. Later, when the ground is frozen hard, they will join other gulls at the refuse tips. There you may well find herring gulls, and even the massive greater black-backed gulls, birds which I normally associate with sea cliffs in the far north.

*Black-headed gulls by Westminster in March; by the end of the month they leave for northern breeding grounds, returning to the city in summer.*

The total number of gulls wintering in the London area is astonishing. In January 1983 a special count was organised by birdwatchers at the main roosts. Unfortunately, the co-ordinated count happened to fall in the middle of a strike by waterworks staff, which meant that some of the reservoirs were closed, so some of the gulls may have gone undetected. Nevertheless they came up with the remarkable figure of 290,901 gulls! Of these, three-quarters were black-headed.

Information from ringing has shown that most of the black-headed gulls come from Holland, Denmark, Scandinavia and countries bordering the Baltic. Their breeding grounds may be as far away as Lithuania or Finland. The lesser black-backed gulls include some from Wales and northern coasts of Britain, but many also come from the far north, from such places as the Faroes, Iceland and Norway. Herring gulls and greater black-backed gulls also come from arctic Norway, but the British herring gulls may originate on the Yorkshire coast and even Guernsey.

Over the past 30 or 40 years the herring gull has grown accustomed to nest in towns and cities all around the coast. No longer is it just a bird of sea cliffs and sand dunes; it commonly chooses rooftops of seaside resorts and, since 1961, at least one pair has tried to nest in central London every year. The Royal Parks and Lords cricket ground have been favourite localities, as well as the rooftops of Whitehall and Westminster. In 1983 a pair nested on the roof of County Hall above my office. For weeks their strident calls echoed around the inner courtyards. One of my colleagues commented on how it reminded him of holidays at Whitby. Another, perhaps less amenable to their noisy displays on the chimneypots, was quite convinced that I had somehow encouraged them; I noticed that his earlier enthusiasm for nature conservation had been somewhat tempered. Breeding was confirmed when a young bird, not yet able to fly, appeared in the Director General's office, having fallen down the chimney.

There are signs that the lesser black-backed gull is also adapting to city life. In the late 1960s several pairs tried to breed in the Royal Parks and, strangely, during the past three years they too have bred at Lords. Forty years ago there was a thriving colony of black-headed gulls at Perry Oaks sewage farm near Heathrow; it gradually dwindled and the last birds bred there in 1964. But this case suggests that the species could easily re-establish itself as a breeding bird if conditions were right.

I wonder what W. H. Hudson would think of this. In *Birds in London*, he describes how the black-headed gulls first became regular winter visitors. Hudson reckoned that they had always visited the lower reaches of the Thames, coming up the river as far as London Bridge. But in the severe winter of 1887–88 they appeared in larger numbers and ranged as far upriver as Putney. He quoted Mr Tristram-Valentine, who wrote:

> 'It is seldom, indeed, that these birds appeared in such numbers in the Thames above London Bridge as they have done lately and their appearance has, from its rarity, caused a corresponding excitement among Londoners, as is proved by the numbers of people that have crowded the bridges and embankments to watch their movements.'

At that time some of the gulls were shot from the bridges, a practice which was stopped by about 1892. In Hudson's view, it was the series of hard winters combined with the new habit of feeding the birds that caused the change. Apparently, in the bad winter of 1893, people would flock to the river during their lunch break to feed the gulls. By the time Hudson wrote his book, five years later, it seems that feeding the gulls in St James's Park had become a regular custom. We still feed them today – and we also provide vast quantities of scraps at the rubbish tips which support a huge winter population. The gulls were quick to learn, and I am sure they will be with us for a long time to come.

## ◆ Canada geese ◆

Visitors to London may be surprised by the flocks of free-flying geese that frequent the central parks. Skeins of 20 or 30 Canada geese can often be seen passing low over the rooftops of Belgravia en route from Battersea Park to the Serpentine or to Buckingham Palace Gardens. On one occasion I saw a large skein flying just above the King's Road in Eaton Square, to the consternation of rush-hour drivers. For me they were a wonderful sight. They bring a welcome touch of wildness to central London.

Strangely, there are some ornithologists who do not give Canada geese a second thought; because they are only introductions, they are thought to be not worth bothering with. But the Canada geese are now as much a part of London as any of the native fauna, and they are a good deal more spectacular than most of our parkland birds. As the name suggests, they are native to North America. They were introduced into Britain over 200 years ago, but it is only very recently that they have become abundant in the London area. A breeding colony of 200 birds was established in 1936 at Gatton Park near Redhill, but there is no record of their occurring further into London at that time. However, birds were released in 1955 in Hyde Park and Kensington Gardens, and ten years later they had spread to four other inner London parks, where they were breeding. Now there are hundreds of them in London. A count in 1983 produced the astonishing total of 2774 birds within 20 miles of St Paul's Cathedral. In that year there were 280 in Hyde Park and Kensington Gardens on 28 June, and 189 in St James's Park in August.

## ◆ Mandarin duck ◆

The mandarin duck is another bird which has now firmly established itself in the London area. This beautiful little duck is a native of eastern Asia, especially China and Japan, but it has long been popular in collections of ornamental waterfowl. It was first brought to Britain in about 1745 by Sir Matthew Decker, a director of the East India Company. He introduced it, along with other exotic species, to his garden in Richmond Green, where it was known as the Chinese teal. A pair bred for the first time in England shortly after the London Zoo acquired them in 1830, and subsequently there have been numerous attempts to establish wild populations; unfortunately, most of these have failed.

It seems likely that most of the birds now breeding in the wild around London originated from a private collection of waterfowl built up by Mr Alfred Ezra at Foxwarren Park near Cobham in Surrey. During the early 1930s birds from this collection spread into the surrounding countryside and a thriving colony developed at Virginia Water near Windsor Great Park. Mr Ezra tried to introduce the mandarin to the central London parks. Nearly a hundred birds were imported from China and set free in various parks and even in Buckingham Palace gardens, but unfortunately the experiment did not work.

However, birds from his collection were more successful elsewhere. They gradually spread along rivers south of Walton on Thames, especially the Mole and the Wey, and by 1951 it was estimated that there were some 400 of them living wild in these wooded river valleys and in woodlands further to the west. Since then the mandarin has continued to spread. Epping Forest has been a popular breeding area in recent years, and now they are nesting in several places within Greater London. One pair bred at Trent Park, and in 1983 a pair even nested in a garden in Southgate. Some of these birds probably came from a collection at Monken Hadley, not far to the west.

All the indications are that mandarin ducks are still spreading and it is possible that, within the next few years, they might colonise wooded parks further into London. A lot will depend on whether they can find suitable nest sites. So far, they have thrived particularly in areas where there are plenty of hollow trees, as at Windsor Great Park and Epping. The mandarin is really a forest bird. Unlike any of our native species, it belongs to a group known as the perching ducks; these birds are quite at home in trees, perching readily on the branches and often nesting in holes high above the ground. In the autumn they feed on acorns, beechmast and chestnuts. Their ideal conditions are where rivers or lakes are overhung by old trees, or where there are secluded ponds within ancient woodland. When disturbed, they fly off remarkably quickly and with great agility through the trees, uttering a sharp high-pitched whistle.

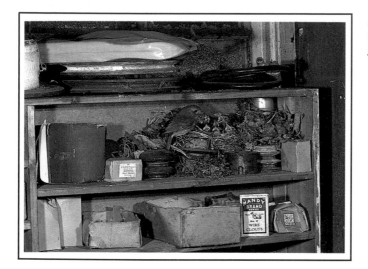

*Some birds thrive in close proximity to man like this robin nesting in a garden shed.* Eric and David Hosking

The mandarins appear to suffer from a shortage of suitable nest holes, and this has sometimes led to overcrowding. In some places, people with gardens backing on to the rivers have provided nestboxes for them. In 1985, one such box was occupied by 3 pairs of ducks at the same time. After their young are fledged, the ducks congregate for their summer moult. A flooded sandpit south of London between Dorking and Reigate is one of their chosen places. By late August in 1983, over 100 had flown in from the valley of the Mole.

The mandarin is certainly a welcome addition to the birdlife of London. With its orange ruffs and chestnut sails, it is a most striking bird. Indeed, it must be one of the most beautiful of all the ducks. No wonder it was cherished as a protected bird for hundreds of years in its native land, where it became a symbol of love and fidelity.

*A pre-roost gathering of starlings on the roof of 10 Downing Street. These birds roost on trees on Duck Island in St James's Park.* David Goode

## ◆ Starlings ◆

Looking across the river from my office window as the sun goes down on a September evening, I often witness one of the most dramatic of all London's wildlife spectacles: the arrival of the starlings. Suddenly over the stately buildings of Whitehall myriads of starlings pour into the city for their nightly roost. Flock after flock fly in over the rooftops from all directions. Each cloud of birds moves purposefully like a distant swarm of bees. But as it passes over Whitehall its momentum is checked and gradually the flock spirals down in wide sweeping movements to the roofs below. There the birds alight in their thousands on every available perch. Their aerial gymnastics look impressive from a distance, but closer to the scene they are even more so.

One evening in mid-September I walked over to Whitehall as the birds began to arrive. It was about an hour before sunset, and as I crossed Westminster Bridge the low sun was casting a golden light on the rooftops. To the west the incoming flocks of starlings were silhouetted against the orange sky. In Whitehall itself, despite the traffic, I could hear the continuous babble of birds on the rooftops, and as I watched still more came spiralling down to join the throng. The greatest congregation seemed to be on the buildings around Downing Street, especially on the side nearest to Horseguards

Parade. The Foreign Office and Cabinet Office were black with birds. Every rooftop ridge and parapet was riddled with chattering rows. Chimneypots, aerials and even the steeply sloping slates of 10 Downing Street itself were covered. Every available chink in the masonry was occupied, including the elaborate stonework of the Royal Insignia on the Foreign Office.

Occasionally, and inexplicably, the birds suddenly fell silent, and a moment later took to the air, a vast throng darkening the sky. But their flight was very brief and soon they settled again on the buildings, only to take up their babbling again with renewed vigour.

A policeman on duty by the back of Downing Street came over to enquire about my interest in the Prime Minister's roof. When I explained that it was the starlings and not the residence that interested me, he took it upon himself to assist by banging vigorously on a metal rubbish bin. This produced a dramatic effect. The whole company of starlings instantly became airborne and nearby tourists took to their heels in fright as droppings rained down. A few minutes later, after the birds had settled again, a kestrel flew low over the Horseguards, whereupon they all took to the wing again in pandemonium. It seemed that the kestrel knew there might be easy pickings here, for it flew among the starlings for several minutes before drifting off across the park.

The policeman told me that the starlings always come at this time of year. He reckoned they would be around each evening for about two months and then they would suddenly disappear. As we talked, I noticed that some of the birds were breaking away from the throng on the rooftops and flying into St James's Park. Gradually more and more followed, until there was a steady stream of birds vacating the buildings.

By now it was dusk and the starlings were moving into their roost at the eastern end of the lake, congregating in their thousands in the willow trees of Duck Island. All around the edge of the lake the trees were full of birds and still they came. For about half an hour there was a constant procession of starlings across Horseguards Parade. With such enormous numbers of birds gathered in so small a space, the clamour was overwhelming. A number of tourists enjoying a summer evening in the park commented in amazement at the spectacle.

As the light faded, a skein of Canada geese flew low along the lake and splashed down noisily. They too were coming in to roost for the night. The pelicans sat huddled on their rocks and ducks already had their heads tucked well beneath their wings.

Duck Island is only one of many central London starling roosts, but during the summer and early autumn it is certainly among the most spectacular. Later in the autumn, as the trees shed their leaves, the birds may abandon the island and move to other roosting places, very likely on buildings. In fact, many of the most famous starling roosts of London are those associated with particular buildings, such as the British Museum, National Gallery and St Paul's Cathedral. Even Nelson's Column has served this function, and on 12 August 1949 a flock of starlings delayed the chiming of Big Ben at nine o'clock in the evening by perching on one of its hands!

In recent years the bright lights of Leicester Square seem to be particularly popular with the birds during the winter months. Not only do they perch on all the available ledges of the buildings, but many persist in using the trees in the centre of the square right through the winter. Unfortunately their droppings cause a mess in the gardens below and every day the park staff have to clean up after them before anyone can use the benches under the trees.

Another favourite roosting place is near St Pancras station, where the starlings gather on a group of gas holders. As they congregate in their thousands on the iron girders high above Camley Street ecology park, they make a fine sight for the children of local schools studying the wildlife of King's Cross.

It is only comparatively recently that starlings have roosted in central London. In 1894 there was a letter in *The Times* pointing out that starlings were flying in to roost in the trees on Duck Island, which seems to have been a new phenomenon. Four years later Hudson described starling roosts on islands in some of the park lakes including Regent's Park, the Serpentine, Buckingham Palace gardens and Battersea Park:

> Before sunset the birds are seen pouring in flock after flock, from all quarters, until the trees on the island are black with their thousands and the noise of their singing and chattering is so great that a person standing on the edge of the lake can hardly hear himself speak.

It seems that Hudson saw this habit developing from the start, for he noted that:

> These meeting-places are evidently growing in favour and if the autumn of 1898 shows as great an increase as those of 1896 and 1897 over previous years, London will have as compensation for its lost rookeries some very fine clouds of starlings . . . At the beginning of October most of the birds go away to spend the winter in the country, or possibly abroad.

Apparently the birds had not yet developed the habit of roosting on buildings throughout the winter. This change occurred some time during the early years of this century and had become a regular custom by the 1920s. Fitter states that:

> By 1922 starlings were roosting all over the central area wherever there were a few trees. The Temple and Savoy Churchyard were said to be the most crowded roosts, and the National Gallery and Nelson's Column were also in use.

What seems to have happened is that birds using the island roosts of the central parks stayed on each year to roost on nearby buildings once the trees had lost their leaves. Perhaps the relative warmth of central London was a sufficient attraction during the winter months, or maybe, as Fitter suggests, their traditional roosts in the countryside had become engulfed in the spread of London so that they were forced to seek roosts within London rather than further afield.

For a long time little was known about where these birds came from, but in 1925 Max Nicholson was able to shed some light on this subject from a rather novel ornithological survey – carried out on open-topped buses. By travelling around London on the upper deck just before dusk, he was able to plot the movements of the starlings as they flew in to the city-centre roosts. He demonstrated conclusively that the huge night-time visitations, totalling at that time some 20,000 birds, were simply a gathering together of starlings which spent the day scattered around the London suburbs. He observed that the birds from particular areas had regular flight lines to the centre. Small groups from the outer suburbs joined up with others en route. So the flocks grew in size to produce the clouds of birds arriving in the central parts.

Since Max Nicholson's pioneering study, there have been many other detailed investigations. Fitter published an account of all the starling roosts of London in the *London Naturalist* of 1942, and there was a three-year study between 1949 and 1957 by the ornithological section of the London Natural History Society. This involved ringing over 5000 starlings either in Trafalgar Square at night or in suburban gardens by day. Recoveries of these ringed birds showed that the majority of those roosting in central London came from the inner and outer suburbs about 6 to 14 miles from the centre. A few birds travelled in from as far away as Epsom, Ruislip, Eltham and Loughton. More recently, the daily flights of starlings into London have even been recorded by radar – producing a dramatic film with the sequence speeded up.

Of course not everyone welcomes the starlings, and there have been many attempts by the City of Westminster, and other local authorities, to find ways of preventing them from roosting in places like Leicester Square. But starlings have been roosting in central London for nearly 100 years now, and it is not easy to control their activities. It may be possible to dissuade them from using a particular roost by using scaring techniques, but they will almost certainly remain somewhere in central London. There is no easy answer and I am inclined to argue in their favour. Their aerial displays are a great attraction and the night-time gatherings on floodlit buildings never cease to evoke wonder and amazement from visitors to the capital. Despite their daily legacy of droppings, they are a feature of London life that I, for one, would be sad to lose.

## ◆ Wagtails ◆

The pied wagtail is a familiar bird of parks and other open grassy places, even in the centre of the city. It can often be seen in the larger squares and has even been known to nest in large suburban gardens. It seems on the whole to be a loner, a small black and white bird constantly on the move, flitting about under parkland trees or running hither and thither on the open grass catching insects. One does not expect to see wagtails in flocks. But outside the breeding season they are more sociable, and you may well spot large gatherings in roosting places.

Although most wagtail roosts in the countryside are in reedbeds, it has long been known that wagtails will also roost in towns – where a particular tree may become a traditional roost. A city-centre roost was described in Dublin in 1931 and several were known in the built-up areas of London during the 1930s. Cramp and others (in *Birds of the London Area*, 1964) refer to a roost of 150 wagtails in holly trees along Balham High Road in 1937 and another in willow trees outside Golders Green station in 1933. Some of these roosts have been occupied for many years. One, in pollarded plane trees along the main London Road in Thornton Heath, first described in 1937 was still in use in 1950.

A study of London's wagtail roosts by Chandler during 1978–79 shows that there were several roosts in the city centre. One of these was in the very heart of the City in plane trees by the church of St Stephen in Walbrook. A congregation of 900 wagtails was assembled in these trees on the night of 3 October 1978. It seems they used this roost throughout the winter, for there were still nearly 500 there the following January. Other roosts were known in plane trees along Buckingham Palace Road and in Hammersmith Broadway. But pride of place for sheer number of birds must go to the Civic Hall at Orpington, where 3025 wagtails were counted going in to roost on 1 November 1978. They had chosen laurel bushes just outside the hall; maybe the popularity of this place has something to do with the thick evergreen bushes which provide cover throughout the winter.

A wagtail roost that I know particularly well is in a small maple tree which stands in the middle of the pavement in a pedestrianised shopping precinct. From late August onwards birds from the surrounding area move into the shopping centre at dusk, where they congregate on the tops of office blocks and shop roofs. Small parties can be seen flying in from all directions to join the throng, and occasionally the whole gathering of birds takes to the air to make skirmishes around the rooftops. Then, when it is almost dark, they drop down into the tree in ones and twos, until eventually there may be 300 wagtails crowded into the single tree. After the leaves fall in November, you can see them at night by the street lamps. They all sit motionless in the crown of the tree, which looks as if it has suddenly produced some exotic winter fruit. Sometimes in winter, when the weather is particularly severe, they forsake their tree and use a holly bush by the bus shelter.

*Pied wagtails roosting in a small maple tree in the middle of a shopping centre. Wagtails have even been known to roost in plane trees in the heart of the city.* Eric and David Hosking

## ◆ Foxes ◆

Of all the recent changes in London's wildlife the colonisation of the capital by foxes is one of the most fascinating. Perhaps this is because the fox seems so out of place in the middle of a large city. After all, it is traditionally regarded as a creature of the countryside. Children's stories would not be complete without crafty Mr Fox paying nocturnal visits to the local farm; braving guard dogs and shotguns, he returns triumphant, with an unfortunate chicken, to his earth, hidden in a secluded copse somewhere deep in the country. There are now large numbers of foxes in London, living cheek by jowl with man, often literally in our own back gardens.

. These foxes are not just visitors from the countryside that have strayed by mistake into town. They were born and bred in the built-up areas of London, and now they are as much part of the urban scene as pigeons or sparrows. You may not see them very often because they are out and about mostly after dark. You may not even realise that foxes live in your neighbourhood. But a conservative estimate suggests that 3000 adult foxes live in Greater London!

This has not always been the case. The evidence suggests that foxes have colonised the built-up areas relatively recently, perhaps only over the past 40 years. When Richard Fitter wrote about the natural history of London in 1945 he said:

> The nearest points to the centre of London where there are still genuine wild foxes appear to be Hampstead Heath, Ken Wood, Mill Hill and Muswell Hill in Middlesex, Epping Forest and Walthamstow in Essex, Elmstead Woods in Kent and Purley, Wimbledon and Richmond Park in Surrey.

All these places have open land or woods, and it seems that at that time foxes had not taken to a more widespread urban existence. Indeed, one implication of Fitter's remarks is that foxes were, if anything, decreasing rather than increasing in London.

In the first half of this century foxes were certainly found in many of the open spaces in the outer suburbs. They were known to local residents around Hampstead by the 1930s; and it is recorded that 116 were shot in Richmond Park between 1931 and 1937. In his fascinating account of the spread of foxes in the London suburbs, in the *London Naturalist* of 1967, Bunny Teagle points out that they were very abundant in some of the outer suburbs in the late forties and early fifties. This claim is backed up by the large number of foxes killed as vermin in the Kentish suburbs during this period. Up to 200 were destroyed each year; and in 1951 on a single day's drive 17 were killed at Scadbury Park near Chislehurst. Further in towards London, John Burton of the London Natural History Society recorded foxes during the late forties at Elmstead Woods, Sundridge Park and on the golf course at Shooters Hill. Perhaps it was from these and other refuges around the fringes of inner London that the foxes colonised the wider range of urban and suburban habitats.

During the 1950s and early 1960s stories started to appear in local papers about foxes being seen much closer to the centre of London. They were turning up in places where they had never been seen before. Bunny Teagle tells how rumours of a fox living in Greenwich Park in December 1961, within six miles of St Paul's, were not taken seriously until it had been seen by several people. Later, several mallard duck died mysteriously in this area and their deaths were attributed to the continued presence of foxes. Late in 1959, the *Willesden Chronicle* contained a photograph of a fox killed on the road in Neasden, and in October 1960 a fox was trapped alive by the RSPCA not far from Vauxhall station – an event reported in *The Times*.

Nowadays such events would not cause great surprise. Foxes are frequently seen in central London, though they seem to be a good deal commoner to the south of the Thames than immediately to the north. It is only the more unusual circumstances that lead to reports in the press. One particular animal caused considerable interest when it had to be rescued from the Thames foreshore near Blackfriars Bridge, where it was cut off by the tide in 1982. Another was reported trotting across Westminster Bridge. In August 1982 the London Wildlife Trust organised a phone-in count of foxes and were amazed when within one month they received reports of over 2000 sightings in London. The peak time for calls on Foxline was three o'clock in the morning. Many of these could, of course, have been duplications, but it still indicates the size of the fox population and the fact that lots of people do see them.

The lifestyle of town foxes has been studied in considerable detail in recent years, particularly by Dr David MacDonald and his colleagues at Oxford University. By catching foxes and fitting them with small radio transmitters, the researchers traced the animals' movements and so discovered all sorts of things about their habits. We now know how far they go to feed, the habitats which they prefer and the kind of places where they lie up by day. It has emerged that each fox has a well-defined territory which is surprisingly small, perhaps only one eighth of a square mile. They favour residential areas, especially detached houses with gardens, as well as areas of woodland and scrub. They also like parkland, golf courses, school and church grounds, as well as disused land for feeding. By day they may go to earth or simply lie up in a secluded spot above ground. The earth of a town fox may be a traditional hole in the ground – plenty of these are dug on railway embankments – but it may equally be under a garden shed or greenhouse, or under a factory building. Quite a number of foxes in London have made their earths under temporary school buildings. As it happens, there is a good supply of food near at hand in such places but this food is not what you might expect: at night the adjacent playing fields provide plenty of earthworms!

Town foxes are opportunistic in their feeding habits. About one third of their diet is obtained by scavenging, including the remains of chicken takeaways, which they will collect from High Street rubbish bins. But about a quarter of their food consists of earthworms and insects, which they find by searching lawns and other grassy places. The remainder is made up of birds, rats, mice, rabbits and hedgehogs. They even eat fruit when it is in season, especially apples and plums.

During the past few years, I have seen foxes in all kinds of places in London, from green-belt woods to a city-centre railway station. In fact they occur so frequently in the city that I am sure I have seen more here in three years than I ever saw while working for many years in some of the wildest parts of Britain! One experience, which I particularly treasure, was the day I unexpectedly came across foxcubs in the middle of a wood at Scadbury Park near Chislehurst. They were tiny creatures, only about six inches long. But their bright little eyes and pricked-up ears compensated for the tiny scrap of tail which would later grow into the characteristic brush. I sat with them for several minutes as they explored crannies among the tree roots. Eventually they clambered over my feet and disappeared into their earth.

Often the only sign of a fox is its smell. Once you are familiar with this pungent scent it is unmistakable – adult foxes use it to mark out their territory. Walk through the old Highgate cemetery and I guarantee that in several places you will be able to pick up the characteristic whiff of fox. Foxes have been living in the cemetery for many years, no doubt ranging over the surrounding gardens and parkland too.

One springtime I visited Queen's Wood near Highgate to listen to the dawn chorus (see Chapter 1). I chose to follow the Parkland Walk along a disused railway line. As I reached Stanhope Road, a fox was picked out by the streetlights as it crossed the street below. It headed for the railway, which no doubt provided a more natural route than the nearby streets. A few minutes later, as I crossed Queen's Wood Road, a second fox came out of the wood and loped away into the nearby allotment gardens. It was still dark and I would not have seen it but for the light of a single lamp-post in the wood. It was an eerie sight. As dawn broke, I sat on a seat in Queen's Wood, listening to the amazing cacophony of birdsong, and yet another fox appeared, trotting nonchalantly along the path in front of me, carrying its 'prey'. As it saw me, it broke into a run and quickly disappeared through the wood. Shortly after that, an early morning dog-walker appeared who told me that he often sees foxes there and that they forage in rubbish bins in Highgate Village.

But you do not have to be up so early to watch foxes. Draughtsmen in offices off Bollo Lane in Chiswick often see the local foxes from their windows; some look forward each year to the time when cubs are born on the Gunnersbury Triangle nature reserve next door. Once, not far from there, a fox walked into Hogarth School one morning during lessons. Fortunately the head teacher was pleased for the children to see it and they all sat watching until it eventually made its way out through the playground. At the Brent Day Field Centre fox-watching is a regular event during the winter. Children there see foxes at very close range, especially during hard weather, when they come right up to the classroom windows to feed on bones put out for them by the warden. At Horniman School, too, the children enjoy occasional visits from foxes. They were sad to find one lying dead in the school grounds after particularly cold weather in January 1985.

Some schools even have their own resident foxes living under the buildings. I know of several cases where local residents have seen them after school hours and become anxious about the dangers of disease or even the unlikely possibility of foxes biting children. One lady, convinced that the school rubbish bins were attracting packs of hungry foxes, contacted the pest officer, who found a pair with several cubs living under the school. Foxes are not like wolves; they do not hunt in packs and it is most unlikely that they would ever congregate to obtain food. Families of foxes under schools are probably a more common occurrence than is generally realised, but they do not actually do any harm.

One evening in late May I was fortunate enough to see a family of foxes at a school in Croydon. There have been foxes at that school since at least 1972, when the present caretaker arrived. They had tunnelled under the concrete edge of the classroom, and the only sign of their presence was a small bone lying outside the hole. As the sun went down, I watched from inside the classroom, which made a perfect 'hide'. The dog fox appeared first, closely followed by the vixen. For a while they sat together on the grass, with the dog fox nibbling the vixen's neck, before they set off together across the playing field. A few minutes later, four well-grown cubs appeared. The caretaker had first seen them about six weeks previously, when they were tiny little cubs. Now they were about 18-inches long and perfect little foxes. They played together like puppies, with a lot of rough and tumble. One, learning to hunt for itself, was foraging in the grass. It pounced on something and, after a little digging, tugged out an earthworm. By now, it was getting dark and the vixen had been gone for a while, but suddenly all four cubs watched intently as she returned across the school field. I think she saw me at the classroom window, for she suddenly barked in alarm and the cubs fled back under the building. The caretaker told me that he had watched the vixen take the cubs out early one morning. She led them across the field, left them sitting together, and then took them one at a time into the adjacent field; she repeated this process with the next fields until she had completed a circuit of the nearby land. He was delighted to have witnessed their first little outing.

Quite the oddest place that I have found foxes is at Broad Street railway station, as already described on page 69. Despite the remarkable array of wildlife I knew existed within the dilapidated station walls, it was still a surprise to find the family of foxes under platform one. One night in 1984 a fox found its way into the Snowshill police station near St Paul's Cathedral. Perhaps it wanted some warmth. The duty policeman was alerted to the intruder on hearing a scuffle in the 'scenes of crimes' office. When he found it was a fox he locked it up and sent for the RSPCA to remove it. I gather that it was 'transported to a more suitable piece of country' and suspect that it had a long walk back to its home in the City.

## ◆ *Badgers* ◆

Some years ago at a nature conservation conference, I remember a lecturer saying 'hands up those who have seen an otter'. A few hands were raised. When the audience was asked if any had ever seen more than one, a lone hand appeared. I am sure that the same would apply to badgers. Have you ever seen one in the wild? If you have not, you are not alone. Even though the badger is such a familiar symbol of wildlife conservation, for many people it is no more than an attractive picture-book animal. As in the case of whales, it is nice to know that they are there, even if we do not see them; but it still comes as something of a shock to find a badger lying dead by the roadside in a London suburb, a casualty of night-time traffic. In fact, badgers are quite plentiful in some parts of London, especially in the south around Croydon and Bromley, where open countryside penetrates furthest into the outer suburbs. I wonder how many of the shoppers in Croydon's busy centre on a Saturday afternoon would believe that badgers can be seen in woods and gardens only two or three miles away.

*A casualty of London traffic.* John Mason

Looking back 100 years or so, it is difficult to find reliable evidence about the status of the badger in the London area. Information is very scanty, but what there is suggests that it was not at all common. The badger had been heavily persecuted and it seems that in many places it had died out almost completely. But during this century its fortunes have improved, probably – as in the case of several bird species – because of the decline in gamekeeping after the First World War. By 1945 Fitter considered it to be quite plentiful in the London area. He wrote that 'on the North Downs in Kent and Surrey the badger still ranks as a common animal even quite near London'. At that time a badger set was known at Ken Wood by Hampstead and Fitter also referred to badgers at Elmstead Woods near Chislehurst.

A detailed survey by the London Natural History Society over five years from 1959 to 1964 showed that, by then, there were quite large numbers of badgers in the London area. Within a twenty-mile radius of St Paul's Cathedral 274 sets were known. Bunny Teagle, who organised the survey (and subsequently published its findings in the *London Naturalist* of 1969), thought that the actual number of sets was probably much greater than this. Some occurred well into the London suburbs, especially where large gardens backed on to open land as at Wimbledon and Richmond. There were several instances elsewhere of badgers being seen in urban gardens, and of sets surviving on private land, such as hospital grounds, which had been surrounded by urban development. In his article in the *London Naturalist*, Teagle referred to badgers living well within the limits of suburbia around Croydon. He went on to mention others which manage to survive even closer to the centre of the capital. Some can still be found near Ham at Richmond, but the most amazing are those which, I am told, inhabit the garden's of the Archbishop's Palace at Lambeth!

In 1966 great prominence was given in local newspapers to a report that the last two badgers in the county of Middlesex had been shot at Bayhurst Wood in Hillingdon – this was shortly after the wood had been designated as a nature reserve. But it was confirmed in 1983 that the animals are still about in this western fringe of London when some suddenly appeared in Uxbridge gardens in midsummer. The badgers' presence was attributed to their displacement by construction of new roadworks along the nearby A40 trunk road. Croydon's badgers have also been in the news recently, with the proprietors of a golf course claiming that they damage the greens; and, more seriously, several cases have come to light of badger digging by people who still promote the illegal practice of badger baiting.

I have been surprised at just how many badgers there are in the southern fringe of London. Tell-tale signs can be seen in many of the woods and along overgrown hedgerows throughout the urban fringe between Croydon and Orpington. Some of the woods have large sets, which are very obvious from the mounds of earth outside the entrance holes. One set that I know well covers over 1000 square yards. It has numerous holes, many of which have fresh red-brown mounds piled outside in springtime. Because the set is on chalkland, each mound is capped by a pile of flints ejected from the burrows. All around are paths through the wood which are regular badger tracks. Though rather narrow, they could be mistaken for footpaths, but one of them leads directly to a fence where it passes through a hole only about one foot high. Often the presence of badgers can be detected from the characteristic black and white hairs caught in such fences along their regular routes.

The hills and valleys of Kenley, Sanderstead and Addington are particularly popular with badgers. One evening in May 1985, I visited one of the sets in this part of London, which is on the edge of a large wood. As I arrived, at about nine thirty, there was a big dog fox snuffling around a nearby pony paddock. The white tip of his tail stood out in the dusk. As he disappeared into the wood, I could just follow his movements as the white spot moved among the trees. I walked quietly through the wood towards the set; it was a good deal darker here than in the open and I had a job to follow the path. As I approached the set, I could make out the shapes of two people standing silently by a tree. Other badger watchers were already there! They were no doubt surprised to see me. Badgers had already been out and, shortly after I arrived, an adult appeared from a hole about 30 yards away. It was followed quickly by a couple of cubs which were about half the size of the adult and a good deal more agile.

As the light faded, other badgers came out until I seemed to be surrounded by their noise and activity. It was difficult to make out what they were up to (only on a later visit did I discover that they are not too disturbed by a torch). They were apparently pulling up the fresh stems of bluebells which covered the area, presumably to use as bedding. Quite often there was the sound of flints cracking together by the entrance holes. Once or twice I heard a deep snapping bark from one of the badgers and occasionally a high-pitched yip from a cub. After about half an hour, the other people having left, I walked quietly over towards the set along one of their runs. Standing absolutely still, I watched the cubs approach to within a few yards. They were rooting out bluebells along the side of the path and occasionally rolling over together in what seemed like play. One of the larger animals stood sniffing with its nose in the air about five yards away. No doubt it sensed that I was there, and eventually it rushed away, taking the cubs with it. I retreated cautiously, leaving the wood to the voices of tawny owls and the intermittent sounds of badgers scuffling in the undergrowth.

A few nights later in the same wood I came across a suspicious-looking group of men equipped with torches, sticks and bags not far from the largest of the sets. I approached them with, I must admit, some trepidation – only to find that they were members of the Badger Protection Society on their nightly rounds. The men seemed to know all the sets in the area and were keeping a watch for badger diggers or the like. Among them was Warwick Reynolds, a leading light in the society who has been watching the local badgers for years. Warwick is a veritable mine of knowledge about London's badgers and seems to spend every waking hour devoted to their protection. He reckons that there must be about 200 of the animals in one square mile of these well-wooded suburbs south-east of Croydon. In this area, many of the residents have become quite used to seeing badgers in their gardens by night. Some regularly put food out for them and look forward to their visits. One man I talked to near Sanderstead regularly spots them in his garden, even though he lives in a row of semi-detached houses, about half a mile from one of the larger woods, totally surrounded by other houses and gardens. He said to me, 'They are creatures of habit. They come out of a night and keep to the same old track from the wood to the end of the lane. Then they go through the gardens. One or two people feed them and if you're around of a night time you'll see them quite often ambling across the road.'

But a badger came as a great surprise to the lady who recently moved into one of the houses on a new estate next to Selsdon Wood bird sanctuary. This badger came into her garden in the middle of the day in December 1984: 'We had some friends round and we all watched it from the window. It came up the steps to the french window and looked right in.' Perhaps it was expecting to be fed. It certainly seems that the population of badgers in this area is artificially high as a result of people putting out food.

With all these stories of badgers in people's gardens, I was keen to see some for myself, so I was delighted when Warwick Reynolds suggested that we visit the house of a Mrs Ward in Sanderstead, where they regularly come for food. Mrs Ward has been feeding badgers outside her back door for about twenty years. Her house backs onto open land near a golf course. Every evening she puts out a pile of syrup sandwiches for them. Even in the winter the badgers come, unless it is very cold. They are such regular visitors that they now have several well-worn tracks through the fence and across the lawn to her back door.

*The first arrival of the evening in Mrs Ward's south London garden.* David Hosking

As we waited, Mrs Ward's cat sat on the window sill watching intently for the first sign of her nightly visitors. The cat is very used to the badgers and will often go out to join them as they feed. Warwick told me of one cat he knows which likes to go down into a set in its owners' garden to sleep.

A large boar was the first to arrive. He surprised us by coming along the side of the garden and appearing suddenly under the window. But he was edgy because of unfamiliar scents and soon ran off. A few minutes later his black and white striped head could be seen again at the foot of the garden. After a brief pause he came quickly towards us with a lumbering gait, swaying slightly from side to side, and making a zigzag course across the lawn. Reaching the path, he gradually nosed his way to the food. Before long he was totally absorbed in licking syrup from the bread. Within minutes others appeared, and soon there were 3 badgers tucking into the pile of sandwiches just outside the window. Mrs Ward could recognise individual animals by slight differences in their markings. One had a rather paler back than the others, while another had darker forelegs.

Most nights Mrs Ward has 3 to 4 badgers coming for food but occasionally in the last year she has seen as many as 8, all trying to feed at once. The first time this happened they all seemed very excited, as if they had gone round to her house for a special treat! On another night she heard a procession of them going along the path past her bedroom 'like a group of children wearing plimsoles'.

As we watched, Mrs Ward switched on an outside light so that the whole scene was illuminated. Suddenly a fox appeared amongst the badgers. He seemed extraordinarily nimble in comparison to the other animals. Quick as a flash he snatched several sandwiches and took them down on to the lawn, where he could eat in relative safety, while the 3 badgers remained prostrate on their bellies, munching their way through the food. They took not the slightest notice when Mrs Ward's cat went out to sit on the low stone wall next to them. This was certainly the most comfortable way to watch badgers.

But, of course, real badger-watching has to be done at a set, and one of the finest sites for this I know in London lies within a small nature reserve run by the London Wildlife Trust on the outskirts of Croydon. It is only a few minutes drive from East Croydon station to a typical suburban road of semi-detached houses with carefully tended front gardens, close-mown grass verges and rows of flowering cherries. It seems an improbable place to find badgers, but behind the houses there is a small wood.

When I went to see the badgers one June evening, I called at one of these houses which is the home of the local London Wildlife Trust representatives. Their garden backs onto the nature reserve. It was simply a matter of walking up the garden path, through a gate into the wood and there was the set! The characteristic mounds of earth were dotted about on a fairly steep sandy slope beneath the trees. One hole which was obviously much used was only a few yards from the back-garden fence. An upturned wheelbarrow lay next to another hole and nearby there was a pile of fresh grass cuttings tipped from the adjacent garden.

Sitting in the wood waiting for badgers to appear, I was very conscious of contrasts. All around were the sounds of children playing in the gardens, someone cutting the lawn with a rotary mower, dogs barking, the jingle of an ice-cream van, and someone appeared briefly at the garden fence to tip over some rubbish. In the wood it was still. Goldcrests sang in the top of tall fir trees and occasionally great spotted woodpeckers called. A pair of grey squirrels suddenly dashed along the boughs of a large beech tree, and high above I could hear the constant chitter of a multitude of house martins as they fed on airborne insects around the canopies of the trees.

Outside the wood, rooftops were still bathed in low sunlight, but among the trees it grew colder as twilight fell. Mosquitoes – the bane of badger watching – homed in to settle on any exposed piece of skin.

The first sign was a nose held high cautiously sniffing the air. Just a momentary glimpse, then it was gone. Like a submarine putting up its periscope to view the surface scene, the badger was testing for any unfamiliar scents in the world up above. Moments later another badger appeared from a hole further up the slope. It stood in the entrance and threw up its head, sniffing. When a second badger tried to come out of the same hole, the first growled and sent it back down inside, itself quickly retreating. A few minutes later the boar emerged again and this time set off at a brisk pace through the wood. He was followed out of the hole by a sow with a couple of small cubs, each about a foot long. They spent quite a time playing together around the entrance hole, rolling over and biting like puppies and kittens. I watched, totally entranced.

By this time, it was getting dark and several badgers appeared all at once from a variety of holes. They stood alert and watchful. Then suddenly it seemed that the wood was theirs and they knew it. Lights were on behind the curtained windows of the houses as I left the badgers to their domain and went back down the garden path into suburbia. I came away with a great affection for these nocturnal creatures who live among us yet are so little known.

Not everyone shares this affection for badgers. Occasionally people find them a real nuisance, particularly if they have a set in their own garden. In July 1985, Mrs Cecily Horsham of Warlingham wrote to the *Croydon Advertiser* about her problems with badgers. When she first moved to Warlingham eight years ago, Mrs Horsham inherited a badger set in the garden, and in her letter she described the first occasion when she saw one:

> On the third night after my arrival here I saw a badger for the first time – a full grown one – from the rear bedroom window. It was a moonlight night and I was fascinated at the sight of this lovely creature.

For several years the Horshams enjoyed seeing the badgers on their nightly visits. Although Mrs Horsham spent a considerable time each autumn clearing the 'rubble' thrown up from the holes, she did not consider the badgers to be a nuisance until the spring of 1984, when there was renewed activity in two holes quite close to the house.

At that point Mrs Horsham took advice from the RSPCA, who referred her to the Ministry of Agriculture, Fisheries and Food (MAFF). An official inspector from the MAFF visited the garden and confirmed that there was a problem as the badgers were nearing the building. Mrs Horsham was advised that the animals should be 'live trapped' and removed, under licence from the MAFF. (Under the 1981 Wildlife and Countryside Act MAFF has responsibility for issuing the licences for control of badgers.)

At first Mrs Horsham followed this advice and applied for a licence. But, on hearing of cases where badgers had been trapped and killed on the spot, she changed her mind and tried other ways of keeping the badgers under control. This included erecting a four-foot-high galvanised chain-link fence around the garden. But, even though the fence extended below ground level, it took the badgers only three days to burrow underneath and regain access to the garden.

Mrs Horsham says that she tried everything she could to keep the badgers out of her garden, all to no avail. Her letter concludes:

> The first act of cruelty to the badgers in Warlingham was perpetrated by the planning department when permission was granted to build houses on the fringe of the wood – cruelty to the badgers and unfairness to the unsuspecting house buyers.

Since her letter was published, Mrs Horsham has had visits from the Badger Protection Society and the Nature Conservancy Council to see if a solution could be found. The badgers had certainly made an awful mess of her garden with their digging, but the main active set lies on adjacent land where the owner wishes them to remain. So, rather than taking steps to remove the badgers completely, the organisations concerned have jointly sought ways of making Mrs Horsham's garden one hundred per cent badgerproof.

Hers was not the only case to appear in the local press that year. Earlier there had been an outcry when the managers of the Selsdon Park Hotel obtained permission from the MAFF to trap and kill badgers which, they claimed, were causing damage to the golf course. A report in the *Croydon News* in January stated that 'according to the hotel, the badgers were damaging the golf course by rooting round for worms and digging holes in the greens'. The entrance holes to the sets were also regarded as a hazard to golfers searching for their balls in the rough. After pressure from the Badger Protection Society, the managers agreed to the badgers being caught and removed to another location. Their destination, as reported in *The Times* of 22 January under the title 'College Badgers', was to be the grounds of Royal Holloway College of London University at Egham in Surrey! Apparently, about 20 badgers had already been caught and removed in recent years from the vicinity of the Selsdon Park Hotel. Most of these were taken to Wimbledon Common, where they were welcomed by the rangers because the local badger population was gradually declining. I doubt whether they would survive there nowadays with all the disturbance, and it raises questions as to whether such introductions are really wise.

After carefully examining the badger sets on Selsdon Park golf course during 1985, the Badger Protection Society concluded that only one set was still occupied – and, in fact, no badgers were caught at all. Nor could any badger damage be detected on the golf course. It was decided that the empty sets should be blocked up to prevent them being reoccupied. This was undoubtedly a wise precaution. With the large population of badgers in this area, it is likely that there will always be some attempting to settle on the golf course. Unfortunately for the managers, it is an ideal habitat for these animals. Maybe instead of trying to eradicate them completely, they should accept the few that remain as a bonus rather than a hazard, and put up notices to warn golfers of badger holes near the remaining set.

With so many badgers in this neighbourhood, odd stories have a habit of surfacing. In August 1984 the *Croydon Advertiser* reported that a badger was rescued after being trapped in a sewer at Selsdon. Mrs Jean Thomas was working in her front garden when she heard a strange noise coming from a drain cover. She took off the cover and found a wet and bedraggled young badger inside. It was totally exhausted and shivering, so she wrapped it up in a blanket and contacted the police. They put her in touch with the Badger Protection Society, which had recently set up a 24-hour rescue service for road casualties. Raymond Ings of the society looked after the badger until it was strong enough to fend for itself and then released it at a set near where it had been found.

Badgers were in the news again in January 1985 when the *Midweek Post* announced that a family of the animals were to be allowed to stay on at Gilbert Scott Junior School where they had set up home in the space under one of the classrooms. A spokesman for the council said, 'So long as they don't start burrowing they can stay.' They are probably still there.

It is not always so easy to cater for badgers in the urban setting. About three years ago there was a proposal to build a block of flats on open land along Park Hill Road in Croydon. Although within half a mile of the centre of Croydon, the place contained several active badger sets, and members of the Badger Protection Society argued strongly against the development. After much discussion the scheme was modified to avoid certain areas occupied by the badgers. But there are problems inherent in such a compromise. Unlike town foxes, badgers cannot get by with a hole under a garden shed. They have a well-developed social structure and strong territorial allegiances. They also require relative seclusion in the vicinity of the set. Once the Park Hill Road development went ahead, there were real doubts about whether the badgers would survive. The Badger Protection Society had done all that it could to argue the animals' case but they knew that the odds were stacked against them. Sadly, the number of badgers has indeed dwindled and, though some can still be seen, the thriving colony of three years ago has gone for ever.

One of the reasons why the Badger Protection Society was first set up in 1979 was because there had been a spate of illegal 'badger digging'. Several of the sets around Sanderstead had been dug out and Jack Martin, a local resident, was so concerned about the onslaught that he gathered together a group to form the society. Since then it has grown from strength to strength. In the 1970s the barbaric practice of badger baiting had suddenly become prevalent in the downland woods around Purley and Selsdon. Terriers were used to flush out the badgers from their sets into nets or bags. I myself have seen on one occasion a group of men in their twenties or thirties with terriers and spades at an active badger set, where they claimed to be controlling foxes.

Badger baiting itself was a nauseating business. A badger was placed in a pit with dogs, but to put it at a disadvantage either its jaw or legs were broken first. Then bets were placed on which would finish off the poor beast. Members of the Badger Protection Society know of several badger-baiting pits in the woods of Croydon and Bromley which were in use as recently as five years ago.

*Badgers at their set.* Ernest Neil

It seems that there has now been a shift away from digging and bagging of badgers to the use of lurcher dogs and lights. In April 1985 two youths from the Coulsdon area were found guilty of killing a badger by using spotlights to set lurcher dogs on it. They had kept the head as a trophy. Each was given a three-month custodial sentence. Jack Martin knows of other cases where people 'go out lamping' at night with lurchers; some have been heard to claim that they set the dogs on anything that moves. Sets have also been interfered with at night by people using nets rather than by digging.

So the badgers in our midst do not have an easy time, and I would not like to judge whether they are holding their ground. In a few places they are well protected, with plenty of people to keep an eye on them. But Warwick Reynolds and his friends cannot keep tabs on all the badgers in south London. They need a lot of help from others who have the interests of the badgers at heart.

# FOUR

# A GREEN
# RENAISSANCE

*Vauxhall City Farm is one of several new inner
city farms in London.* David Goode

STANDING BY KEN WOOD high on Hampstead Heath and enjoying the magnificent view over Parliament Hill Fields to the distant skyline of the City, it is easy to forget the battles fought in the nineteenth century to protect this much loved landscape, and many other commons and open spaces, from the tide of new development sweeping out from London. Hampstead had an early taste of such problems even in the eighteenth century when commoners opposed to new houses on the heath provoked a riot. From 1830 onwards pressure grew in earnest as the lord of the manor, Sir Thomas Wilson, put a procession of bills to Parliament seeking permission to enclose the heath and build houses on it. At each attempt he was thwarted by the strength of local feeling and especially by the long-established rights of commoners. Yet he persisted in what he believed to be his rights over the heath.

The year 1865 was crucial for the future of London's open spaces. At that time disputes affected not only Hampstead but also Epping Forest, Wimbledon and many other commons on the fringe of the urban area. So serious were the issues that a select committee was appointed by the House of Commons to inquire into the best means of preserving, for the use of the public, the commons, open spaces and forests in the neighbourhood of London. What had previously been a series of individual cases now achieved much wider significance. At the same time that Tom Willingale, a commoner of Epping Forest, was fined for lopping trees – a protest on his part against the lord of the manor, who was illegally preventing the commoners from exercising their rights over a large part of the forest – some of those most involved with protecting Hampstead Heath, such as George Shaw-Lefevre, were instrumental in forming the Commons Preservation Society. This new society played a leading role in the subsequent protection of both Hampstead Heath and Epping Forest. By 1871 Hampstead Heath and Wimbledon Common were saved. That year marked the beginning of a lawsuit brought by the Corporation of the City of London against those responsible for enclosing Epping Forest. Because the City had bought a small plot for a cemetery within the bounds of the forest it had claim to commoners' rights over the whole forest and was able to contest the recent enclosures. Ably supported by the Commons Preservation Society, the City won the case, and promptly bought out the interests of the lords of the manors. Since the Epping Forest Act of 1878, the forest has been used for the free enjoyment of the people of London. The City even reinstated the old Court of Verderers and was able to remove some of the piecemeal enclosure that had already taken place.

This period was remarkable for the way in which local people joined forces and organised themselves to save their common inheritance. Of course they were not the first to do so. In 1630 local inhabitants protested that Leicester Fields should not be taken from them for new houses. Their success lives on: a fragment survives today as Leicester Square – though I doubt that the original protestors would recognise it now. A few years later the residents of Lincoln's Inn protested about proposals to build houses on Lincoln's Inn Fields. The Society of Lincoln's Inn insisted in 1638 that the fields be kept as a public park with walks, in the same manner as Moorfields. Despite their influence as lawyers, the society failed to win that battle, though parts of the fields have survived. It was at about that time, too, that opposition was raised against Charles I for his plans to enclose Richmond Park – though in the event his action resulted in protection of one of the most remarkable open spaces in London.

The protection of open spaces has taken many forms. During the latter part of last century, following the closure of all the City burial grounds in 1852, there was a move to turn all the graveyards into parks and squares. Octavia Hill, later active in establishing the National Trust, was one of the main protagonists of this movement. She wanted to keep the small graveyards as open spaces for people to enjoy: 'open-air sitting rooms for the poor'. This enthusiasm led to the formation in 1882 of the Metropolitan Public Gardens Association, which was responsible for protecting nearly 500 churchyards, many of them being turned into tiny parks or gardens. These areas still provide a sense of sanctuary in many parts of central London.

*The bird sanctuary on Hampstead Heath. Fenced off from the public it provides a refuge where reed buntings, sedge warblers, herons and even kingfishers may be seen.*

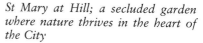

*St Mary at Hill; a secluded garden where nature thrives in the heart of the City*

During the Victorian expansion of London there was an enormous demand for new parks and open spaces. The strength of popular feeling was well illustrated in 1840 when 30,000 people in Tower Hamlets signed a petition asking the government for a new park in London's East End. Four years later work started on Victoria Park, and it is said that, on one day in 1846, 20,000 people visited the unfinished park. Other parks followed, at Battersea, Kennington and Finsbury, setting the fashion for the now familiar formal layout of a Victorian park. It should not be forgotten that much of the pressure for the parks' creation came from local people.

Today the fight to protect open spaces of all kinds continues. There are innumerable local protection societies in London, many of which are remarkably powerful, among them Crouch End Playing Fields Protection Society, Friends of Nunhead Cemetery, the Brent River Preservation Society and Friends of Holland Park.

There is, however, one difference in the modern picture: the appreciation of the natural world has gradually taken on a greater significance. We are now witnessing a period of enthusiasm and vigour comparable with the 'open-spaces' movement of the Victorian era, but the present vigour stems, no longer simply from a desire to protect open spaces for human enjoyment, but from people's needs in relation to the natural world.

The protection of Selsdon Wood and Perivale Wood as bird sanctuaries early this century was one of the first steps in a move towards nature conservation. So too was the creation of a bird sanctuary at Walthamstow Reservoir in 1923. The London

Natural History Society drew attention to the value which this reservoir might have as a bird sanctuary, but at that time it was still used by private shooting parties. A combined approach to the Metropolitan Water Board by the Royal Society for the Protection of Birds (RSPB) and the Selborne Society was successful. Shooting was stopped and the reservoir has been managed as a sanctuary ever since.

Such progress was well in advance of its time. Though the RSPB had existed since 1889 and the Society for Promotion of Nature Reserves was established in 1912, it was not until after the Second World War that organised nature conservation got properly under way in Britain, with the setting-up of the Nature Conservancy and the gradual build-up of county-based trusts. The result in London, as elsewhere, was the protection of areas of special quality either as nature reserves or by designating them Sites of Special Scientific Interest. Interestingly, such places in London included from the outset a number of totally artificial habitats. Reservoirs are a good example: the value of Barn Elms, Walthamstow and the Welsh Harp Reservoirs has been recognised for many years.

But there has recently been a fundamental change of emphasis. No longer is it only the special places with rare or unusual species which are thought to merit protection. We have moved into a new phase of nature conservation which is more concerned with the value of ordinary wildlife to townspeople in the places where they live. I could choose many examples to illustrate this phenomenon, but for me the turning point came with a small wood in west London known as Gunnersbury Triangle.

It all started late in 1981, when a resident of Chiswick Road opened her bedroom curtains one morning to find that some of the birch trees on the other side of the railway line had been felled by heavy machinery. The trees were on a piece of unused railway land which had been isolated long ago by a triangle of railway tracks. For years it had been left virtually undisturbed. But now Anne Mayo was worried. Some years earlier, one edge of the triangle had been developed for offices and warehouses. Now it looked as if there might be plans afoot for other new developments. The triangle of woodland was the only genuinely wild place for miles around. It even had willow warblers nesting – Anne Mayo could hear them from her garden – and the family of foxes that lived there was well known to local people.

Enquiries at the local planning offices and with British Rail revealed that there were indeed suggestions that the seven-acre site could be developed for warehousing. So far no official application had been made, but the sight of the machinery removing trees to carry out test drilling was enough for Anne Mayo to act. Urgent discussions were held at the Hounslow Borough offices and a tree preservation order was served on British Rail to prevent any further destruction of the woodland. Nevertheless the land had been identified in the local plan as suitable for future development, and it was clear that some of the officials were very doubtful about the nature conservation arguments.

I became involved in Gunnersbury in July 1982, when Alfred King, the leader of Hounslow Council, asked for a second opinion on the triangle's ecological value. So, shortly after joining the Greater London Council as its ecologist, I visited the triangle with a colleague, David Hope – and with Anne Mayo, who had by that time made the place famous by talking about it on John Craven's *Newsround* and on several other television and radio programmes. We had obtained permission from British Rail for the visit, and Anne was pleased to accompany us officially as until that time she and her colleagues in the recently formed Chiswick Wildlife Group had been unable to gain such permission. But in spite of the permission, access that day and for many months to come was by scaling a high wire-mesh fence: a hazard typical of those to which I have since become accustomed while poking round London's unofficial wildlife sanctuaries.

As we dropped down into the wilderness of birch and willow trees and tramped through the lush summer growth of vegetation, there was a remarkable tranquillity about the place. District Line tube trains rattled past on one side, and the occasional train on the North London line, but despite these the woodland had a quiet of its own. A small copper butterfly was basking in the sun along the disused railway track, and there was a profusion of flowers in the open glades and along the woodland ride. Water plantain was flowering alongside celery-leaved crowfoot in a small marshy patch. One of the rarer plants we saw was hemlock water dropwort, another plant of marshes and river banks. In the trees several willow warblers and a blackcap were singing and I was surprised to hear the flight song of a lesser redpoll so far into the centre of London.

We were later to discover that the whole woodland had grown up over the past 40 years. I found it hard to believe that a wood with so natural a feel about it could have come about within my own lifetime. Yet aerial photographs taken in the early 1940s indicate that only a few scattered trees existed at that time.

Walking through the wood that day, I was quickly convinced that a good case could be made for its protection. The Chiswick Wildlife Group had already produced an excellent booklet advocating that the triangle should be a nature reserve. This had generated a lot of local interest, and there was obviously substantial support for the proposal. Once I had seen the inside of the triangle, I did not need much convincing. I advised the borough of my view. By that time some of the councillors were taking the nature conservation proposals very seriously and were keen to negotiate directly with British Rail.

Several meetings followed between the borough and representatives of British Rail, with the Chiswick Wildlife Group and myself providing the ecological arguments. All to no avail. BR was not willing to drop proposals for development of the site. Jointly with Lovell's Developments Ltd, it planned to extend warehousing over the whole of the triangle. Obviously it was in BR's interest to obtain the best possible income from the site; with planning permission for development, its value could have been well over £1 million. So, despite a great deal of pressure from the borough, several public meetings and a very considerable outcry against any development, BR and the developers nevertheless decided to go ahead. A formal planning application was submitted early in 1983.

The Borough asked whether, if it turned down the application, I would act on its behalf as expert witness at a public inquiry. Even at that stage, it seemed, some of the staff were not convinced that they had firm grounds for refusal of planning permission. Nevertheless it was refused, and the public inquiry was held in July 1983.

This inquiry was significant in a number of ways. It did not depend on traditional nature conservation arguments, but on the attitude of the community. The strength of local opinion and the value of the place to local people mattered more than the detailed factual evidence regarding the wildlife content of the triangle. This seemed to take the developers and the ecologists working for them by surprise. In their view, the triangle was a rather nondescript piece of derelict railway land which had little merit for nature conservation. They argued that it was not exceptional in any way. It had no rare species to speak of. It was too small to be effective as a nature reserve. It was not particularly rich in species, and anyway most of them were likely to be found elsewhere in the vicinity. Nor was it an ancient habitat. On the countrary, it had been in existence for only 40 years. It had none of the features which, in traditional nature conservation terms, would make it a place worth preserving.

But there were two other crucially important factors which the developers had ignored: the triangle was the only sizeable piece of natural habitat of any kind for miles around, and it was surrounded by a large number of people.

At a packed evening session of the inquiry in Chiswick Town Hall, local residents spoke with feeling about the value of having a piece of nature in their midst. Railway commuters spoke too, commenting on how it was their only contact with the 'countryside' on their journey to work. One elderly lady who lived close to the triangle spoke movingly about the birch trees which for her were a real link with nature, unlike anything else that she saw in her confined city life. When she stepped down from the stage, she was given a rapturous ovation. In a few halting words she had captured what so many people felt.

But there was more technical evidence too. Jan Hewlett of the Chiswick Wildlife Group had brought together a formidable team of experts on various aspects of the triangle's natural history and they were able to demonstrate very forcibly its value as a local nature reserve. This was also the basis of my argument: not that it was an outstanding area for wildlife, but that it provided the only opportunity to study and experience wildlife at first hand in the area. Much of the evidence concerned the triangle's future use by schools for nature study, and for this there was powerful support from local teachers.

A month after the inquiry the inspector announced his decision: the development should not be allowed because of the considerable local ecological value of the site. The outcome was hailed as an important precedent for urban nature conservation and will no doubt be quoted at many other public inquiries up and down the country. Anne Mayo was, of course, delighted, but there was still a long way to go before all the potentialities of a nature reserve could be fulfilled. It was another year before the land was bought from British Rail by the Borough of Hounslow, aided by a grant of £58,000 from the Greater London Council. There was an amusing side to that, because the grant was given under powers for the creation of local nature reserves under the National Parks and Access to the Countryside Act of 1949. Gunnersbury Triangle in the heart of Chiswick has provided its own bit of countryside, and now the public indeed have access to it. The Chiswick Wildlife Group formally took over management of the nature reserve at an opening ceremony on 29 March 1985. The willow warblers missed the opening by a few days but several were singing all through April and May and now they can be appreciated by a much larger audience.

Gunnersbury Triangle is only one of many recent battles fought in the cause of nature conservation. A few years ago a vigorous and successful campaign was mounted to save the Walthamstow Marshes; the group who spearheaded it produced an inspiring booklet which made a most convincing case for protection of the 'fen in the city' for local people to enjoy. Another case was Wilderness Island on the River Wandle near

Hackbridge, which local residents fought to keep wild. Then there was the Parkland Walk in Haringey along the disused railway track from Finsbury Park to Alexandra Palace: plans for housing along the railway were dropped after a public inquiry in 1978, largely on account of the variety of birdlife to be seen along this walk. A series of decisions in favour of nature conservation following public inquiries on the future of Crayford Marshes, Sydenham Hill Woods and islands in the Thames at Brentford all show that wildlife conservation in urban areas has become thoroughly accepted.

Local authorities in London are now making provision for nature reserves when planning the urban environment. Parts of the Welsh Harp Reservoir are likely to be designated as an official Local Nature Reserve. For many years there have been only two such reserves in London. Now another 20 are under consideration by councils. Most heartening is the fact that some boroughs are establishing official ecology committees as part of their planning departments, and a new joint committee is continuing the ecological work of the GLC.

The idea of town nature reserves, particularly for the use of schools, is not new. Local educational nature reserves were proposed in 1947 by the government's wildlife conservation committee chaired by Sir Julian Huxley. It was recommended that such reserves 'should be made available at least to all the large centres of population so that they can be used by schools'. It took some 30 years for that message to find effect. But recently a number of nature study centres have been set up in various parts of London on all kinds of unused land. The Welsh Harp Day Field Centre has been operating since 1973 on land originally purchased for use as a cemetery, and the chapel was converted

Left *The ponds by Caesar's Well at Keston in Bromley are popular with children for fishing; they also contain a rich variety of aquatic life including some uncommon dragonflies.*
Below *Reedbeds along the canal at 'Tump 53' in Thamesmead, a nature centre which was developed on one of the moated islands of the old Woolwich Arsenal. Additional reedbeds have been created.* David Goode.

to a makeshift classroom. Another centre is based in a cemetery at St Mary Magdalene church in Newham. There are others at Beckenham Place Park in Lewisham and Capel Manor in Enfield. Some of the most effective reserves are quite small. One is the Litten Nature Reserve in Ealing. It consists of only three acres, with a few old oaks, some hedges and a pond, but it is a wonderful place for children. Another is the Devonshire Road Nature Reserve along a railway embankment in Lewisham. All these new nature reserves are extremely popular with local primary schools.

At Devonshire Road I met a party of children aged about ten or eleven from Horniman School who were out birdwatching with the head teacher Mrs Abbott. She regularly takes small groups there, and on this particular day they watched a kestrel hunting and learned to identify the songs of various warblers, including chiffchaffs and blackcaps. One group found a slow-worm sunning itself on the bank: that was the highlight of the day. For Mrs Abbott the greatest value of this wild patch is that it can be reached in a few minutes' walk from school. Several of her group had become so keen that they had already joined the Young Ornithologists Club. This nature reserve has been such a success that the Borough of Lewisham has now promoted other such sites, also on unused railway land, as they provide almost the only open spaces in this heavily built-up part of London.

There are now teams of people from the British Trust for Conservation Volunteers, the Urban Spaces Scheme and several other groups devoted entirely to developing local plots for use by schools. The vision of the Huxley committee has at last come to fruition.

The sudden burgeoning of school nature reserves is symptomatic of something which goes much deeper: a new ethos towards wild in the city. Over the past few years we have witnessed a tide sweeping through London as local people have taken action to re-establish their links with countryside, wilderness and all that is green. Concern for nature plays a large part in this ethos, but it has just as much to do with promoting community gardens and city farms as with the protection of wildlife. The green renaissance is not something imposed by officialdom; it is a grassroots movement of the dispossessed. People have become divorced from the natural world, yet they recognise their need for it.

The action has taken many forms. Gardens have been created by local community groups on undeveloped building plots, such as the aptly named 'Meanwhile Gardens' in Paddington or the attractive Phoenix Gardens in a back street off Tottenham Court Road. Volunteers have capitalised on derelict land to develop the city farms which have sprung up in the most unlikely places over the past ten years. Local children spend hours mucking out stables and feeding pigs at Vauxhall City Farm only a few minutes' walk from Westminster. Another example is Stepping Stones Farm, which has all the familiar farm animals, including cows, on a tiny patch right in the middle of the crowded streets of Stepney. An even more unlikely spot for a farm is a disused wharf by the Thames downstream of Rotherhithe, but quite the most extraordinary is Mudchute Farm on the Isle of Dogs. Once a dumping ground for silt dredged from the nearby Millwall Docks, the Mudchute's hillocks now support a 30-acre farm and park. Since it was opened in 1977, this farm has gradually built up a wide selection of livestock and now has 80 pigs, 70 sheep, 12 cows, 8 goats, several types of geese, ducks and turkeys, and a stableful of riding ponies which are even used for rounding up the sheep. Highlight of the year is the Isle of Dogs Agricultural Show held at the Mudchute every

June. But it isn't only a farm. The Eastend Wildlife Group is actively encouraging a greater variety of wildlife at the Mudchute by planting appropriate shrubs and trees. Already they have been rewarded by the arrival of beautiful yellow brimstone butterflies, which have established themselves on the newly planted alder buckthorn. This wildlife group is busy in other parts of the East End too, promoting nature conservation in places such as Tower Hamlets Cemetery and St Jude's Nature Park near Bethnal Green. Not only Tower Hamlets but several of the other cemeteries mentioned earlier are now being managed as nature reserves.

The past few years has seen an enormous growth in the number of volunteers involved in wildlife conservation in the capital. The London Wildlife Trust, though only established in 1981, now has over 3000 members with groups in every borough and a mammoth programme of activities. As well as fighting to save particularly important places like Sydenham Hill Woods, the trust advises on the management of all kinds of valuable wildlife areas, such as the Glebelands in Barnet, Battersea Park, the Regent's Canal and the disused filter beds at Lea Bridge Road. It has published a guide for parks staff on how to encourage wildlife in urban parks and has organised a successful series of events in which the public can participate, such as 'foxwatch' and 'owl-prowl'. Currently the Trust is aiming to set up at least one nature reserve in each of the 33 London boroughs.

The British Trust for Conservation Volunteers is another rapidly growing organisation with a huge army of volunteers dedicated to practical conservation tasks. At weekends, groups are out digging ponds, planting trees, coppicing ancient woodland, laying hedges, putting up fences, building paths and even cutting hay — all within the boundaries of the metropolis. One group included someone who worked weekdays at the Stock Exchange and wanted 'some fresh air and contact with nature at the weekend'. He was immersed up to his waist planting a new reedbed in the Regents Canal behind King's Cross station.

The importance of nature to city inhabitants brings a new dimension to conservation. No longer is it sufficient to protect the outstanding vestiges of the natural world such as Ruislip Woods or Wimbledon Common, however important they may be; nor even the best of the man-made wild such as the Welsh Harp Reservoir or Nunhead Cemetery. Something more is required if people are to have greater contact with nature in their daily lives. But imagination and creativity are needed for this to be achieved. Much can be learned from the unofficial wild spaces where nature has already found accommodation in our midst. Looking at the city with new eyes, one realises that there is a multitude of exciting possibilities which have yet to be taken advantage of.

In 1976 Max Nicholson (see page 123) suggested the creation of an 'ecology park' on the south bank of the Thames by Tower Bridge as part of the Silver Jubilee celebrations. His idea was to establish, as cheaply as possible, a small area of natural vegetation on what was at that time a vacant plot used as a lorry park. I suspect that few of those concerned had the slightest notion what form the ecology park would take; it was a completely new idea so far as London was concerned. Nevertheless, just over two acres of land were made available on a peppercorn rent for five years, on the understanding that the park would eventually disappear when the proposed Thameside development went ahead. In this way the William Curtis Ecological Park was born.

A plan was drawn up in November 1976 indicating the range of habitats to be created, including a small meadow, mixed woodland, osier beds and a shallow pool. Construction was entirely by volunteers who broke up the hardcore of the lorry park and spread subsoil obtained by the simple device of advertising the site as an inner-city subsoil dump. Nearly 150 different species of plant were introduced, as appropriate to the various habitat types; they included a spinney of birch trees and other patches of alder, aspen, willow and hazel.

The shallow pond, illustrated on the front cover of the book, was an immediate success. Some of the plants introduced around the margins spread quickly to produce a remarkably natural feel, with beds of softrush, great willowherb, reedmace and bur-reed. The yellow-flowered greater spearwort, which is fast becoming a rarity in its native bogs and fens, also spread vigorously and had to be weeded out. Water mint and marsh dock flourished and, in the water, bog bean, water milfoil, and white waterlilies formed a continuous mat of vegetation full of aquatic insects.

The rate of colonisation at the William Curtis Park exceeded expectations. Even within the first two years the plant life of the park had increased dramatically. By 1980, 348 different sorts of plants had been recorded. Some were early colonisers which then disappeared; others came at a later stage, and gradually the habitats were enriched by growths of clover and vetches. After only four years 27 species of leguminous plants had colonised the grassland of the park.

Frogs were introduced to the pond early on and were remarkably successful. By 1980 foxes and a hedgehog were recorded, and the hedgehog droppings were found to contain the remains of a great variety of insects. In fact, by that year, surveys of the invertebrate fauna of the park, referred to by local schoolchildren as 'minibeasts', revealed nearly 200 species of which only 5 were known to have been deliberately introduced. They included 25 species of spiders, 63 different sorts of moth and 35 beetles. Although only three years old, the pond already attracted 6 different kinds of dragonfly, including the largest of our native species, the bright blue emperor dragonfly.

Butterflies too had increased dramatically. Indeed, of all the changes at William Curtis Park, colonisation by butterflies is probably the most powerful demonstration of what can be achieved in the middle of a huge city. In the first year after the new habitats were created, 6 species were seen, all of them common and predictable in central London. They included small tortoiseshell, peacock and meadow brown. The following year a further 6 species were seen, 4 of which occurred in all subsequent years: the common blue, wall, Essex skipper and speckled wood. The next year saw 4 more additions. So the increase continued, and by 1984 21 species of butterflies had been recorded, 16 of which had been seen consistently in the previous three years. The gradual increase over the years was dependent on the progressive establishment of a rich grassland with nectar- yielding trefoils and vetches.

The park was a great success with local schools. It was not long before it was booked solidly by classes through every term. In eight years the entirely artificial habitats of William Curtis Park played host to over 100,000 visitors, providing insights into the natural world never before available to children in central London. For some it was a very special place which they will remember all their lives.

When the time came for redevelopment of the site, many of these children felt a great sense of loss. In the weeks before it finally closed in July 1985, their first question on arriving at the park was: 'What are we going to save today?' There was a constant procession of children taking trees, plants, frogs and 'minibeasts' to places of safety in nearby school grounds, parks and gardens. At the time of writing the park has still not been built over and in early April 1986 local children took it upon themselves to mount a further rescue operation for frogs and frogspawn in the pond, carrying bucketsful to nearby ponds.

William Curtis Park paved the way for other more permanent nature parks in central London. In May 1985 the GLC opened a new ecology park at Camley Street by the canal at the back of King's Cross station. This two-acre plot was a disused coalyard when I first saw it in 1982. Now it is a most attractive place, with a large pond and reedbeds fringed by birch and willow trees, and there is a small nature study centre. During January 1986 a heron came down each evening to roost on the marsh, giving its stamp of approval to this newly created habitat.

The park at Camley Street is now managed by the London Wildlife Trust and has proved to be enormously popular with local schools. A full-time teacher is based there, paid for by the Inner London Education Authority, and two wardens are funded by the borough of Camden. Camley Street has made history as the first artificially created nature park to be designated as an official Local Nature Reserve.

The reedbeds of Camley Street provide a clue to what might be done in other parts of London. If a habitat suitable for herons can be successfully established so near King's Cross, the possibilities are endless. Bringing nature into the everyday life of townspeople is a practical proposition. Opportunities exist to create new habitats and encourage wildlife in all sorts of places; some imagination is needed to make the most of them, but it can be done and there is plenty of enthusiasm from local community groups to ensure that new schemes are carried through.

*Camley Street park, opened in May 1985, is fully booked by local schools for ecological studies. Here children are pond dipping.*

*Dean's Yard, Westminster. Ivy-covered walls show what is possible on buildings. New buildings in the capital could be designed to provide new habitats for plants, birds and insects as a means of encouraging wildlife.*

Ecology parks and nature gardens are only a start. If buildings are considered as potential habitats, a whole series of opportunities is opened up. For example, inner-city bee-keepers would benefit from rooftop heather gardens, which could provide a marvellous food source for honeybees. Roof gardens planted with low-growing shrubs and herbs could provide new 'aerial ecosystems' for city wildlife. I have seen blackbirds feeding young on a tiny patch of rooftop lawn beside a penthouse flat seven stories up in Baker Street. Blue tits nest in small rooftop gardens and other birds could be encouraged. The resident blackbirds poking for worms in window boxes at the London Ecology Centre above the traffic of Shelton Street in Covent Garden are an indication of things to come.

I would go further and actively encourage wildlife by including habitats within the design of new buildings. Shrubs and small trees can be grown in courtyards and on balconies. Architects have sometimes incorporated gardens in buildings to improve their visual appearance, but more could be achieved if the needs of wildlife were also taken into account. Special bricks with holes in for bats are now available. Nest boxes for kestrels could be automatically included in the building of high office blocks. Designing for wildlife gardens in new housing schemes could become a normal part of community architecture.

The days when linnets and goldfinches were collected in the countryside and sold by the thousand as cage birds in the East End are long since gone. But the need for people to have something of the natural world in their midst is just as strong today as it has been in the past. The future bodes well for wild in London.

# BIBLIOGRAPHY

Barker, F., and Gay, J., *Highgate Cemetery, Victorian Valhalla*. John Murray: Friends of Highgate Cemetery, London.

Burton, R. M., *Flora of the London Area*. London Natural History Society, 1983.

Chandler, R. J., 'Pied wagtail roosts and numbers in the London area in winter', *London Bird Report* No. 44. London Natural History Society, 1979.

Dixon, C., *The Bird-life of London*. Heinemann, London, 1909.

Emery, M., *Promoting Nature in Cities and Towns*. Croom Helm, London, 1986.

Farmer, A., *Hampstead Heath*. Historical Publications, New Barnet, Herts, 1984.

Fitter, R. S. R., *London's Natural History*. Collins, London, 1945.

Fitzgerald, P., *London City Suburbs*. Leadenhall Press, London, 1893.

Flint, R., *Clapham Common Nature Walk*. London Wildlife Trust, 1984.

Greater London Council, 'Ecology and nature conservation in London', *Ecology Handbook 1*. GLC, London, 1984.

Greater London Council, 'A nature conservation strategy for London; woodland, wasteland, the tidal Thames and two London Boroughs', *Ecology Handbook 4*. GLC, London, 1986.

Hadden, R. M., 'Wild flowers of London W1', *London Naturalist* No. 57. London Natural History Society, London, 1978.

Holmes, B., *The London Burial Grounds*, 1896.

Homes, R. C., 'Twenty-five years of Duck Counts in the London Area', London Bird Report 39, London Natural History Society, 1974.

Hudson, W. H., *Birds in London*. Longman, London, 1898.

Jefferies, R., *Nature Near London*. 1883.

London Natural History Society, *The Birds of the London Area*. Hart-Davis, London, 1964.

Lousley, J. E., 'Mitcham Common and its conservation'. Proceedings of Croydon Natural History and Scientific Society No. XV. 1971.

Ministry of Works, *Birds in London*. Report by the Committee on Bird Sanctuaries in the Royal Parks (England and Wales) 1939–1947, HMSO, London, 1948.

Montier, D. J., *Atlas of Breeding Birds of the London Area*. Batsford, London, 1977.

Penry-Jones, J., 'Selsdon Wood Nature Reserve'. Proceedings of Croydon Natural History and Scientific Society No. XVI. 1978.

Silvertown, J., 'The history of woodlands in Hornsey', *London Naturalist* No. 57. London Natural History Society, London, 1978.

Teagle, W. G., 'The fox in the London suburbs', *London Naturalist* No. 46. London Natural History Society, London, 1967.

Teagle, W. G., 'The badger in the London area'. *London Naturalist* No. 48. London Natural History Society, London, 1969.

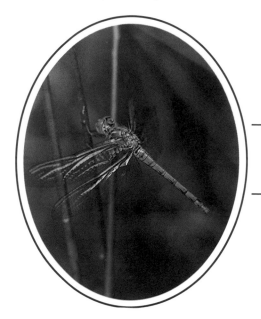

# INDEX